MW00812526

Boston Slave Riot, and Trial of Anthony Burns: Containing the Report of the Faneuil Hall Meeting, the Murder of Batchelder, Theodore Parker's Lesson for the Day, Speeches of Counsel On Both Sides, Corrected by Themselves, a Verbatim Report of Judge Loring

Fetridge And Company

Nabu Public Domain Reprints:

You are holding a reproduction of an original work published before 1923 that is in the public domain in the United States of America, and possibly other countries. You may freely copy and distribute this work as no entity (individual or corporate) has a copyright on the body of the work. This book may contain prior copyright references, and library stamps (as most of these works were scanned from library copies). These have been scanned and retained as part of the historical artifact.

This book may have occasional imperfections such as missing or blurred pages, poor pictures, errant marks, etc. that were either part of the original artifact, or were introduced by the scanning process. We believe this work is culturally important, and despite the imperfections, have elected to bring it back into print as part of our continuing commitment to the preservation of printed works worldwide. We appreciate your understanding of the imperfections in the preservation process, and hope you enjoy this valuable book.

E, TWENTY-FIVE CENTS.

THE
BOSTON SLAVE RIOT,
AND
TRIAL
OF
Anthony Burns,

CONTAINING THE

**REPORT OF THE FANEUIL HALL MEETING; THE MURDER OF
BACHELDER; THEODORE PARKER'S LESSON FOR THE DAY;
SPEECHES OF COUNSEL ON BOTH SIDES, CORRECTED
BY THEMSELVES; VERBATIM REPORT OF JUDGE
LORING'S DECISION; AND, A DETAILED AC-
COUNT OF THE EMBARKATION.**

BOSTON:
WILLIAM V. SPENCER.
1854.

Press of J. S. Potter & Co. 2 Spring Lane and 101 Washington Street.

B 0

BOSTON SLAVE RIOT,

AND

TRIAL

OF

ANTHONY BURNS.

*Burns died at Sweetburnes,
Canada West, where he was pastor of a
church on the 27th of July 1862, in
the*

CONTAINING THE *Twenty fourth*

of his Magum 186?)

REPORT OF THE FANEUIL HALL MEETING; THE MURDER OF BATCH-
ELDER; THEODORE PARKER'S LESSON FOR THE DAY; SPEECHES
OF COUNSEL ON BOTH SIDES, CORRECTED BY THEMSELVES;
A VERBATIM REPORT OF JUDGE LORING'S DECISION; AND
DETAILED ACCOUNT OF THE EMBARKATION.

BOSTON:
FETRIDGE AND COMPANY.
1854.

218 M
37-6

8371 ~~23~~

U.S,5311.8

BOSTON SLAVE RIOT

April 12

The Gift of

Rev Thomas Wentworth Higginson

of

Worcester Mass

TRIAL OF ANTHONY BURNS,

THE ALLEGED FUGITIVE SLAVE.

THE ARREST.

On Wednesday evening last, about eight o'clock, Anthony Burns, colored, while walking in Court street, was taken into custody by officers Coolidge, Riley, and Laighton, under the orders of Watson Freeman, United States Marshal, and by virtue of a warrant issued by United States Commissioner Edward G. Loring, authorizing the arrest of Burns, as an alleged fugitive from the "service and labor" of Charles F. Suttle, a merchant of Alexandria, Va. The arrest was made very quietly, and he was escorted to an upper room in the court house, where, under a strong guard of officers, he was kept for the night, and the intelligence of his arrest did not transpire until the following morning.

Burns, who is about thirty years old, has for some time been in the employ of Coffin Pitts, clothing dealer, No. 36 Brattle street. He is a shrewd fellow and his story of the manner of his leaving Alexandria is curious. After acquitting his master of all suspicion of cruelty, he stated that leaving him was the result of accident — that one day, while tired, he laid down on board a vessel to rest, got asleep, and that during his slumbers, the vessel sailed! Burns, at one time after his arrest, expressed a willingness to return with his master, but he was induced by his advisers to make his claimants show their authority for his return.

THE EXAMINATION.

On Thursday, at nine o'clock, the United States Marshal made return of his doings to the Commissioner, who proceeded to investigate the case. Messrs. Seth J. Thomas and Edward G. Parker appeared as counsel for the claimants, and Messrs. Richard H. Dana, Jr., Charles M. Ellis and Robert Morris volunteered as counsel for the alleged slave. The official papers — embracing the customary powers of attorney, &c., from the court in Alexandria — having been read, Mr. Parker read the complaint, of which the following is a copy : —

United States of America, Massachusetts District, ss

To the marshal of our District of Massachusetts, or to either of his deputies.
Greeting.

In the name of the President of the United States of America, you are hereby commanded forthwith to apprehend Anthony Burns, a negro man, alleged now to be in your District, charged with being a fugitive from labor, and with having escaped from service in the State of Virginia, if he may be found in your precinct, and have him forthwith before me, Edward G. Loring, one of the Commissioners of the Circuit Court of the United States for the said District, then and there to answer to the complaint of Charles F. Suttle, of Alexandria in the said State of Virginia, merchant, alleging, under oath, that the said Anthony Burns, on the twenty-fourth day of March last, did, and for a long time prior thereto had owed service and labor to him, the said Suttle, in the State of Virginia, under the laws thereof; and that while held to service there by said Suttle, the said Burns escaped from the said State of Virginia into the said State of Massachusetts; and that said Burns still owes service and labor to said Suttle, in the said State of Virginia, and praying that said Burns may be restored to him, said Suttle, in said State of Virginia, and that such further proceedings may then and there be had in the premises as are by law in such cases provided. Hereof fail not, and make due return of this writ, with your doings thereto, before me.

Witness my hand and seal, of Boston aforesaid, this twenty-fourth day of May, in the year one thousand eight hundred and fifty-four.

EDW. G. LORING, Commissioner.

United States of America, Boston, Massachusetts District ss., May 25, 1854.

Pursuant herewith, I have arrested the within named Anthony Burns, and now have him before the Commissioner within named, for examination.

WATSON FREEMAN, United States Marshal.

The first witness introduced was William Brent, who deposed as follows:—

I reside in Richmond, Virginia, am a merchant; have resided there four years; know Mr. Charles F. Suttle—he now resides in Alexandria; he is a merchant; know Anthony Burns; now see him at the bar in front; he is the man referred to in the record which has been read; he is owned by Mr. Suttle as a slave; he was formerly owned by Mr. Suttle's mother; Mr. Suttle has owned him for the last twelve or fifteen years. I have hired Anthony of Mr. Suttle; this I think was in the years 1846, 1847 and 1848; paid Mr. Suttle for his services. I knew that he was missing from Richmond on or about the 24th day of March last; have not seen him since until a day or two past. Last night I heard Anthony converse with his master.

Mr. Dana here took occasion to say that he had not been regularly retained as counsel, and he addressed the Commissioner as follows:—

May it please your Honor: I arise to address the court as *amicus curiæ*, for I cannot say that I am regularly of counsel for the person at the bar. Indeed, from the few words I have been enabled to hold with him, and from what I can learn from others who have talked with him, I am satisfied that he is not in a condition to determine whether he will have counsel or not, or whether or not and how he shall appear for his defence. He declines to say whether any one shall appear for him, or whether he will defend or not.

Under these circumstances, I submit to your Honor's judgment that time should be allowed to the prisoner to recover himself from the stupefaction of his sudden arrest, and his novel and distressing situation, and have opportunity to consult with friends and members of the bar, and determine what course he will pursue.

Mr. Parker. I feel bound to oppose the motion. The counsel himself says that the prisoner does not wish for counsel, and does not wish for a defence. The only object of delay is to try to induce him to resist the just claim which he is now ready to acknowledge. The delay will cause great inconvenience to my client, the claimant, and his witness, both of whom have come all the way from Virginia for this purpose, and will be delayed here a day or two if this adjournment is granted. If it were suggested that the prisoner were insane, out of his mind, and would be likely to recover soon, we could not object. As it is we do object.

Mr. Dana replied. The counsel for the prosecution misapprehends my statement. I did not say that the prisoner did not wish counsel and defence. I said he was evidently not in a state to say what he wishes to do. Indeed he has said that he is willing to have a trial. But I am not willing to act on such a statement as that. He does not know what he is saying. I say to your Honor, as a member of the bar, on my personal responsibility, that from what I have seen of the man and from what I have learned from others who have seen him, that he is not in a fit state to decide for himself what he will do. He has just been arrested and brought into this scene, with this immense stake of freedom or slavery for life at issue, surrounded by strangers — and even if he should plead guilty to the claim, the Court ought not to receive the plea under such circumstances.

It is but yesterday that the Court at the other end of the building refused to receive a plea of guilty from a prisoner. The Court never will receive this plea in a capital case, without the fullest proof that the prisoner makes it deliberately, and understands its meaning and his own situation, and has consulted with his friends. In a case involving freedom or slavery for life, this Court will not do less.

The counsel for the claimant objects to a delay; he objects on the ground of the inconvenience to which it will put the claimant and his witness, who have come all the way from Virginia for this purpose! I can assure him, I think, that he mistakes the character of this tribunal, by addressing to it such an argument as that. We have not yet come to that state in which we cannot weigh liberty against convenience and freedom against pecuniary expense. We have yet something left by which we can measure those quantities.

I know enough of this tribunal to know that it will not lend itself to the hurrying off a man into slavery to accommodate any man's personal convenience, before he has even time to recover his stupefied faculties, and say whether he has a defence or not. Even a suggestion from an *amicus curiæ*, the Court would, of its own motion, see to it that no such advantage was taken.

The counsel for the claimant says that if the man were out of his mind, he would not object. Out of his mind! Please your Honor, if you had ever reason to fear that a prisoner was not in full possession of his mind, you would fear it in such a case as this. But I have said enough. I am confident your Honor will not decide so momentous an issue against a man without counsel and without opportunity.

Mr. Ellis urged the postponement on the ground of the importance of the issue. Commissioner Loring informed the prisoner that he was entitled to counsel, and that if he desired it, time would be given to afford him an opportunity to select them. Burns, who seemed somewhat amazed, at length muttered that he desired delay, and the further hearing of the case was thereupon postponed until Saturday morning. The usual order was issued to the Marshal to keep the prisoner in a place of safety, and the Court then adjourned.

THE PUBLIC MEETING.

The interest felt in the slave was very general, but the leading abolitionists obtained the use of Faneuil Hall for Friday evening and issued the following card, which appeared in all the papers and was placarded throughout the city.

A MAN KIDNAPPED. — A Public Meeting will be held at Faneuil Hall this (Friday) evening, May 26, at 7 o'clock, to secure justice for a man claimed as a slave by a Virginia kidnapper, and imprisoned in Boston Court House, in defiance of the laws of Massachusetts. Shall he be plunged into the hell of Virginia slavery by a Massachusetts Judge of Probate?

In the evening an immense concourse of people filled the hall, and the meeting was called to order by Hon. Samuel E. Sewall, and it was organized as follows: —

George R. Russell, of Roxbury, *President.*

Vice Presidents — Samuel G. Howe, William B. Spooner, Francis Jackson, Timothy Gilbert, F. W. Bird of Walpole, Rev. Mr. Grimes, Albert G. Browne of Salem, Gershom B. Weston of Duxbury, T. W. Higginson of Worcester, Samuel Wales, Jr., Samuel Downer, Jr.

Secretaries — William I. Bowditch and Robert Morris.

On taking the chair, Judge Russell said, he had once thought that a fugitive could never be taken from Boston. But he had been mistaken! One had been taken from among us, and another lies in peril of his liberty. The boast of the slave holder is that he will catch his slaves under the shadow of Bunker Hill. We have made compromises until we find that compromise is concession, and concession is degradation. (Applause.)

The question has come at last whether the North will still consent to do what it is held base to do at the South. Why, when Henry Clay was asked whether it was expected that Northern men would catch slaves for the slave holders, he replied, " No! of course not! We will never expect you to do what we hold it base to do." *Now,* the very men who had acquiesced with Mr. Clay, demand of us that we catch their slaves. It seems that the Constitution has nothing for us to do but to help catch fugitive slaves!

When we get Cuba and Mexico as slave States — when the foreign slave trade is reëstablished, with all the appalling horrors of the Middle Passage, and the Atlantic is again filled with the bodies of dead Africans, then we may think it time to waken to our duty! God grant that we may do so soon! The time *will* come when Slavery will pass away, and our children shall have only its hideous memory to make them wonder at the deeds of their fathers. For one I hope to *die* in a land of liberty — in a land which no slave hunter shall dare pollute with his presence. (Great applause.)

Dr. S. G. Howe then presented a series of resolutions, which set forth that the trial on Saturday was an outrage not to be sanctioned, or tamely submitted to —

That as the South has decreed, in the late passage of the Nebraska bill, that no faith is to be kept with freedom; so, in the name of the living God, and on the part of the North, we declare that henceforth and forever, no compromises should be made with slavery. That nothing so well becomes Faneuil Hall as the most determined resistance to a bloody and overshadowing despotism. That it is the will of God that every man should be free; we will as God wills; God's will be done! That no man's freedom is safe unless all men are free.

Mr. Francis W. Bird of Walpole, late Chairman of the Free Soil State Central Committee, counselled "fight."

Mr. John L. Swift said: — " Burns is in the Court House. Is there any law to keep him there? The fugitive slave law received in the House on Tuesday night one hundred and thirteen stabs — and was killed. The compromises are no more — they were murdered by the Nebraska bill. Hereafter let not the word compromise desecrate the tongue of any true American. It has been said that Americans and sons of Americans are cowards. If we allow Marshall Freeman to carry away that man, then the word cowards should be stamped on our foreheads. (Cheers.) When we go from this cradle of liberty, let us go to the tomb of liberty, the Court House. To-morrow Burns will have remained incarcerated there three days, and I hope to-morrow to witness in his release the resurrection of liberty. This is a contest between slavery and liberty, and for one I am now and forever on the side of liberty."

Wendell Phillips said he was glad to hear the applause to this sentiment, that the city government is on our side. If the city police had been ordered on the Simms case as they are now not to lift a finger in behalf of the kidnappers, under pain of instant dismissal, Thomas Simms would have been here in Boston to-day. To-morrow is to determine whether we are ready to do the duty they have left us to do. (Cheers.) There is now no law in Massachusetts, and when law ceases the people may act in their own sovereignty. I am against squatter sovereignty in Nebraska and against kidnappers' sovereignty in Boston. See to it that to-morrow in the streets of Boston you ratify the verdict of Faneuil Hall that Anthony Burns has no master but his God.

The question, he said, was to be settled to-morrow whether we shall adhere to the result of the case of Shadrack or the case of Simms. Will you adhere to the case of Simms, and see this man carried down State street between two hundred men? (No.) I have been talking seventeen years about slavery, and it seems to me I have talked to little purpose, for within three years two slaves can be carried away from Boston. Nebraska I call knocking a man down, and this is spitting in his face after he is down. When I heard of this case and that Burns was locked up in that Court House, my heart sunk within me.

See to it, every one of you, as you love the honor of Boston, that you watch this case so closely that you can look into that man's eyes. When he comes up for trial get a sight at him — and don't lose sight of him. There is nothing like the mute eloquence of a suffering man to urge to duty; be there, and I will trust the result. If Boston streets are to be so often desecrated by the sight of returning fugitives, let us be there, that we may tell our children that we saw it done. There is now no use for Faneuil Hall. Faneuil Hall is the purlieus of the Court House to-morrow morning, (cheers) where the children of Adams and Hancock may prove that they are not bastards. Let us prove that we are worthy of liberty.

Theodore Parker next spoke, and after some fiery remarks he called the people "fellow subjects of Virginia," which he said he would take back, when they accomplished deeds worthy of freemen. He said that one of the officers of the city government told twenty policemen to-day not to lift a finger in support of the slave catchers, and the order was received with cheers. Mayor Smith was invited to preside at this meeting, and he said he regretted that his time was all engaged this evening so that he could not come. His sympathies, he said, were all with the slave. They think they can carry Burns off in a cab (Voice — They can't do it; let them try it.)

Mr. Parker then proposed that when the meeting adjourn it adjourn to meet in Court Square to-morrow morning at 9 o'clock. A hundred voices cried out, "no, to-night," "let us take him out," "let us go now," "come on," and one man rushed frantically from the platform, crying "come on," but none seemed disposed to follow him. Mr. Parker— "Those in favor of going to-night will raise their hands." About half the audience raised their hands. Much confusion ensued, and the persons on the platform seemed bewildered and in hesitancy how to control the excitement they had raised. The audience were shouting and cheering — a voice was heard saying "the slave shall not go out, but the men that came here to get him shall not stay in: let us visit the slave catchers at the Revere House to-night."

After a while sufficient order was restored to allow the chairman to put the questions on the resolutions, and they were passed unanimously — and it was moved to adjourn. Again cries of "to the Court House" and the "Revere House" were heard. The scene was tumultuous in the extreme. At last Wendell Phillips again took the platform, and said:

Let us remember where we are and what we are going to do. You have said to-night you will vindicate the fair fame of Boston. Let me tell you you won't do it groaning at the slave-catchers at the Revere House — (We'll tar and feather them) — in attempting the impossible feat of insulting a slave-catcher. If there s a man here who has an arm and a heart ready to sacrifice any thing for the freedom of an oppressed man, let him do it to-morrow. (Cries of to-night.)

If I thought it could be done to-night I would go first. I don't profess courage, but I do profess this: when there is a possibility of saving a slave from the hands of those who are called officers of the law, I am ready to trample any statute or any man under my feet to do it, and am ready to help any one hundred men to do it. He urged the audience to wait until the day time; said that he knew the vaults of the banks in State street sympathized with them; that the Whigs who had been kicked once too often sympathized with them. He told them that it was in their power so to block up every avenue that the man could not be carried off. He urged them not to balk the effort of to-morrow by foolish conduct to-night, giving the enemy the alarm. You that are ready to do the real work, be not carried away by indiscretion which may make shipwreck of our hopes.

The zeal that won't keep till to-morrow will never free a slave. (Cries of "No!")

Mr. Phillips seemed to have partially carried the feelings of the audience with him, when a man at the lower end of the hall cried out — "Mr. Chairman, I am just informed that a mob of negroes is in Court square, attempting to rescue Burns. I move we adjourn to Court square."

The audience immediately began rapidly to leave the hall, and most of them wended their way to Court square.

THE ATTEMPTED RESCUE AND LOSS OF LIFE.

The crowd moved from Faneuil Hall to the Court House, and halting on the East side endeavored to force the door on that part of the building, but failing in their attempt they ran round to the door on the West side opposite the Railroad Exchange, with loud cries that the fugitive was in that wing of the building, and there proceeded with a long plank, which they used as a battering-ram, and two axes to break in and force an entrance, which they did, and two of their number entered the building, but were quickly ejected by those inside. The battering-ram was manned by a dozen or fourteen men, white and colored, who plunged it against the door, until it was stove in. Meantime, several brickbats had been thrown at the windows, and the glass rattled in all directions. The leaders, or those who appeared to act as ringleaders in the melee, continually shouted: "Rescue him!" "Bring him out!" "Where is he!" &c. &c. The Court House bell rung an alarm at half past nine o'clock. At this point reports of pistols were heard in the crowd, and firearms, we understand, were used by those within the building, but whether loaded with ball or not we cannot say. During this struggle some thirty shots were fired by rioters, and the most intense excitement prevailed. The whole square was thronged with people. The Chief of Police, Taylor, was upon the ground with a full force of the Police, to stay the proceedings of the mob, now pressing still more reckless and threatening. Mr. Taylor pressed through the excited multitude, and, with great heroism, seized several men with axes in their hands, while breaking down the Court House door.

At the time the mob beat down the westerly door of the Court House, several men, employed as United States officers, were in the passage-way, using their endeavors to prevent the ingress of the crowd, and among the number was Mr. James Batchelder, a truckman, in the employ of Colonel Peter Dunbar, who, almost at the instant of the forcing of the door, received a pistol shot, (evidently a very heavy charge,) in the abdomen. Mr. Batchelder uttered the exclamation, "I'm stabbed," and falling backwards into the arms of watchman Isaac Jones, expired almost immediately. The unfortunate man resided in Charlestown, where he leaves a wife and one or two children to mourn his untimely fate.

At the time of forcing the door, and just as the fatal shot was fired, one of the rioters who was standing on the upper step, exclaimed to the crowd, "You cowards, will you desert us now!" At this moment, the exclamation of Mr. Batchelder, "I'm stabbed!" was heard, and the rioters retreated to the opposite side of the street.

In the meantime a white man rushed into the crowd and distributed several meat axes, with the blades enveloped in the original brown papers. Two or three of these axes were subsequently picked up by the officers, and were deposited in the Centre Watch House.

After the arrests had been made, the crowd, although excited, remained quiet, but a new element was introduced by the arrival of a military company. The Boston Artillery, Captain Evans, were in the streets for their usual drill. When they marched up Court street, the mob at once supposed them to be the United States Marines, come to preserve order; and they were at once saluted with hisses, groans, and other marks of derision. Captain Evans seeing an excited crowd, and not knowing any thing of the disturbance, immediately marched his men down the West side of the Court House, and halted in the square, the crowd giving way. When the cause of the appearance of the company was explained, the crowd gave them three cheers, and the company departed.

A large force of officers were detailed for duty during the night outside the Court House, and throughout the whole evening and night an additional strong force was inside, fully armed for any emergency.

During this scene, the judges of the Supreme Court, the Attorney General of the Commonwealth, and the Sheriff of Suffolk were in the building awaiting the return of the jury in the Wilson case, who were to come in at 11 o'clock. Some members of the jury, who put their heads out of the window to see what was going on, were fired at, and the balls in one or two instances, struck quite near them. The windows of the Justice's court room were completely riddled by bullets discharged from without.

Marshal Freeman had a very narrow escape, a ball having struck the wall quite near him, while he was leading his men up to repulse the individuals who had broken in. His son was present and displayed great courage.

During these outrages upon the Court House, the Chief of Police summoned his men to protect the peace in the square, and with the assistance of only five men, rushed into the crowd before the door, and succeeded in arresting and bearing off to the watch house, the following persons:

A. G. Brown, Jr., American, 23 years of age, riotous conduct; John J. Roberts, American, 25 years of age, breaking a gas lamp in the square; Walter Phinney, colored, 36, and John Wesley, colored, 26, riotous conduct; Wesley Bishop, 30, colored, disturbing the peace; Thomas Jackson, 42, colored; Henry Howe, 22; Martin Stowell, 30; John Thompson, 27, for disturbing the peace.

The Mayor was notified by his Chief of Police of the state of affairs, and he at once issued an order on Colonel Cowdin for two companies of artillery. At twelve o'clock the Boston Artillery, Captain Evans, and the Columbian Artillery, Captain Cass, came to the aid of the civil authorities. Their presence served to restore quiet, and Court Square was soon deserted by the rioters. Captain Evans's command was stationed in the City Hall for the night, and Captain Cass's company took quarters in the Court House. At half past twelve o'clock the square was deserted.

The Boston Artillery numbered 40 guns, and the Columbian Artillery appeared in full ranks.

During all this while there were three or four carriages standing in Court square, all of which were closely watched by the crowd, for fear that Burns might be secretly brought from the Court House, and suddenly driven off. At one time a number of persons started off from the square with the intention, as we infer from their language and remarks, to drum up assistance for further operations later in the night.

Prominent among the crowd were seen the leading speakers at the meeting in Faneuil Hall.

During the tumult, a number of our most respectable citizens called at the police office, and tendered their services to assist in maintaining peace and order. Their offer was accepted.

No determined effort was made by the mob to rescue the arrested persons, but several partial rushes were made in the direction of the officers. The crowd being urged on by their leading spirits.

The windows on the west side of the court house are nearly all broken, and the door on that side torn from its hinges.

Captain Morrill states that when he rushed into the crowd to make arrests, several pistols were fired upon him, some of them evidently being loaded with ball; fortunately he was uninjured.

After the door had been forced open, John C. Cluer attempted to effect an entrance, but was repulsed by the officials, and after demanding admittance "as a citizen of Boston," made a few blustering remarks and left.

The noise of the mob created a stampede in the Museum, and much alarm prevailed among the ladies. The performances were interrupted, and nearly half the audience left the house.

The murder was not generally known by the mob, and when it was stated that a man had been shot, one of the ringleaders of the rioters replied, with great emphasis, "Then there will be one the less to kill to-morrow."

The murderer of Batchelder contrived to make his escape. He can, however, be identified by several persons. One of the reportorial corps saw him shoot the deadly weapon. We hope ample justice will be rendered.

Albert G. Brown, Jr., of the Law School, who was arrested, is a son of A. G. Brown, of Salem, a member of Governor Boutwell's council. His friends promptly offered bail for his appearance this morning, which was refused.

A few persons loitered about the court house through the night, but no disturbance occurred after the melancholy affair in the fore part of the evening.

Between 12 and 1 o'clock last night, Deputy Marshal Riley proceeded to East Boston, and calling up the Captain and Engineer of the steamer John W. Taylor, chartered that boat for special service. Steam was got up with despatch, and the boat proceeded at once to Fort Independence, when she took on board a corps of United States Marines, under command of Major S. C. Ridgley and Lieutenants O. B. Wilcox and O. A. Mack. She then returned to the city, and at half past six o'clock this morning the troops were quartered within the walls of the Court House.

About the same hour that Mr. Riley left for East Boston, Officer W. K. Jones was despatched to the Navy Yard in Charlestown with orders for troops, and in a very short time a corps of United States Marines, numbering 50 men, rank and file, under command of Lieutenant Colonel Dulaney, with Captain J. C. Rich, 1st Lieutenant Henry W. Queen, 2d Lieutenant A. N. Balser, were also quartered in the Court House, and reported to the United States Marshal as ready for duty.

THE EXCITEMENT ON SATURDAY.

At an early hour in the morning, those interested, with hundreds of idlers, gathered around the Court House, and at an early hour the Independent Corps of Cadets, Lieutenant Colonel T. C. Amory, and the Boston Light Infantry, received orders from Major General Edmands to assemble at their armories, and then to report themselves at City Hall. A detachment of the Boston Light Dragoons, Company B, were also in readiness at their armory, and a corporal's guard at each of the armories.

The body of the unfortunate officer Batchelder, who fell a victim to the unrestrained passions of the mob last night, was removed by order of Coroner Smith, to his late residence in Charlestown. As the coffin was being placed in the covered carriage which conveyed it out of the Square, the noisy outcries of the assembled multitude were hushed, and quiet reigned until the vehicle which bore the body had left the Square. An inquest will be held on Monday.

When other vehicles passed through the Square, the violently disposed were quite boisterous, and crowded upon the officers who were stationed about the easterly entrance of the Court House. Three or four of the most forward in these disturbances were promptly arrested and committed to the Centre Watch House. These summary arrests tended to cool the ardor of the rioters, and order was once more restored for a time.

In company with High Sheriff Eveleth, Mayor Smith appeared on the steps of the easterly entrance of the Court House, and, being introduced by the Sheriff, as the Mayor of the city, briefly addressed the crowd. He expressed regret at the assemblage, and warning the multitude, as good and peaceable citizens, to quietly go to their homes, at the same time adding, that a sufficient force was in readiness to preserve the public peace; and that, at all hazards, the laws of the city, the laws of the State, and the laws of the United States, SHALL be maintained. (Applause.) Again beseeching the crowd to disperse quietly, and go to their several residences or places of business, and remarking that in case they remained, they might be presumed to do so for no good purpose, his Honor retired, and, in company with the Sheriff, repaired to the City Hall.

Just as the Mayor closed his remarks, a colored man made some demonstration of disrespect, and he was immediately arrested and committed to the Watch House. A large number of the more orderly portion of the crowd soon retired.

The following are the names of the persons arrested this forenoon: Charles H. Nichols, George Smith and Edward D. Thayer, (minors,) James Nolan and John Jewell, (adults,) and William Johnson, (colored.) The last named is the one who, at the close of the Mayor's address, made a disrespectful and insulting remark.

The Mayor caused posters to be printed, bearing the following request, which were posted throughout the city.

To the Citizens of Boston:

CITY HALL, Boston, May 27, 1854.

Under the excitement that now pervades the city, you are respectfully requested to coöperate with the Municipal Authorities in the maintenance of peace and good order.

The laws must be obeyed, let the consequences be what they may.

J. V. C. SMITH, Mayor.

THE EXAMINATION OF BURNS.

Saturday morning the examination of the alleged fugitive slave Anthony Burns, was resumed before United States Commissioner Edward G. Loring, Esq., in the United States District Court room. At five minutes past nine o'clock, the prisoner was brought in under a strong guard and placed in the dock. The officers of the Marine corps and a large number of spectators were present.

Edward G Parker and Seth J. Thomas, Counsel for the government, Richard H. Dana, Jr., and Charles M. Ellis, Esq., Counsel for defence.

At quarter past ten, Mr. Parker proposed to proceed. Mr. Ellis moved for further delay to afford time for greater preparation of the case. He said the law ought not to be executed till a case had been made out as clear as daylight and free from all cavil or doubt. It was not till yesterday afternoon that he or Mr. Dana felt at liberty to act as counsel for the prisoner. None except himself had been allowed to see the prisoner; he did not know whether this exclusion had been by order of the Court or not. As none had been permitted to see him and as he did not feel at liberty to act as his counsel till a late hour yesterday, it was the same as if the prisoner had been seized yesterday. There was another reason for delay; he did not think men could act calmly and in a manner to serve justice, under the existing circumstances. He had not believed that such a train of circumstances could ever occur here again, but such was not the fact. He asked the Court to consider that it was the sole obstacle between the man and perpetual Slavery. Under the United States law, there is no process known to the law that can now interpose. There is more reason that a magistrate should be able to say, " I have given you time for the amplest preparation and my mind is free from bias and prejudices from influences within or without." There is no man who has heard what has been done who can say that it is a cause for proceeding—but on the contrary is a sufficient cause for delay. He again urged continuance in view of the excited state of public feeling. He said he thought there was power enough to secure order, and that the trial could proceed in an orderly and lawful manner. Force begets force, and he thought that nothing could be gained by haste.

Mr. Parker replied that he hoped there would be no delay, and for reasons which must be obvious to every mind. He thought that sufficient delay had already been granted. The ground he took was that this was but the preliminary examination which was by no means final. No further time could tend to show that the record is incorrect, or objectionable in itself. The Court in view of the excited state of feeling should expedite the proceedings.

Seth J. Thomas, Esq., rose and said that as the defence had moved for delay, he proposed to consider the nature of the case, the motion for delay, and the reasons in support of that motion. He related the circumstances of the connection of the Counsel for defence with the prisoner. He admitted that at first the prisoner was not in a frame of mind to determine what to do.

" If there is," said he, " a law whereby my client has property in this man, and this claim is made out, there is but one thing to be done by the magistrate, —a certificate is to be made out and the prisoner is removed; the question of servitude or freedom is to be determined by the state to which he is carried. The Court sits here to try the proofs of the claim." He then considered the reasons alleged in support of the motion. He understood from the Marshal that on the first application to see the prisoner he had refused, but had afterwards consented. He believed that the prisoner had no defence to make to the claim. When the Court asked the prisoner the other day with whom he had conversed, he answered with no one except his "master" and one other, thus admitting that he was held to servitude. He could not see any ground in an ordinary case for continuance; no facts could be elicited to disprove the claim. The Court has seen what has occurred here, and if certain gentlemen can lay their heads upon their pillows and say that the blood of that man is not upon them then he should be glad to hear it. He hoped that the opposing Counsel were not of the number of those men. His client had letters from very respectable people in the State from which he comes; he says that one Anthony Burns who owes him servitude has escaped, and asks if there is any means to take him back to the State from which he escaped. That claim is like a promissory note, and why should there be any more opposition than in such a case if the claim be proved. Gentlemen may not like the law, but it is nevertheless the LAW. The inevitable effect of continuance would be that the excitement without would be increased. Can it be said that this law is inoperative and cannot be enforced; is it any the less treason to attempt to take away this and resist the law of the United States than it is to go to the other end of the court room and rescue the man who has been tried and found guilty of murder. He could see no reason urged for continuance which was not an objection to the law rather than to the administration of the law.

Mr. Dana said the counsel for claimants had urged objections to the motion drawn from politics, philanthropy, and every thing else except a sound and direct answer. Shall the prisoner be hurried into a trial immediately, or shall proper delay be granted ? They had not asked half as much delay as there was in the Simms case. He narrated the circumstances of the arrest of Burns. The prisoner had been taken to the court house, which for two years had been occupied not as a jail—he wished he could say as much—but as a *slave-pen*. He was happy to bear witness that the Court had called the prisoner up, perceiving that he was intimidated, and counselled him in a parental manner, advising him of his legal rights. It was not till after a written order had been passed by the Court, that any body beside himself had been *permitted* by the Marshal to see the prisoner, and it was within the last 24 hours that it was ascertained whether he wished Counsel or not; had it not been for the *order* of the Court, it would not probably have been till this time. This was sufficient ground for delay, but there was another reason.

Yesterday afternoon a hearing was had before Judge Sprague, on an application for replevin of the man to carry the case before another magistrate; at half past six o'clock the decision was given, refusing the application.

The argument against delay, that violence would issue, was not a proper ground — it was a confession of weakness.

"Had that man," said Mr. Dana, "been born under the same roof with your Honor, and fostered by the same hand, this record, made up *ex parte,* would be sufficient to show that he was born in Virginia, even though the affidavit be made up in the testimony of a single man." He therefore urged delay, inasmuch as the act of this Court could not be revised, even by the Supreme Court of the United States. This is not a case of extradition, and the prisoner goes to no other court; he is given to the man who calls himself his master, and in his custody he remains. The claimant is not bound to take him to Virginia; he may take him to Texas, the coast of Africa, or New Orleans, to a slave mart.

The court ruled that the reasons set forth were sufficient grounds for delay till Monday. In regard to the excitement, he regretted it; it seemed to him that the request was by no means unreasonable, and would therefore delay till Monday morning, at 11 o'clock.

The court then adjourned. During the examination, a guard of marines were posted along the passage ways, and on the stairs, presenting a formidable appearance. Nothing like disorder was manifested.

ATTEMPTED ARREST OF SUTTLE.

During the forenoon, a writ was issued by Seth Webb, Esq., on an action of tort, for the recovery of $10,000 damages against Messrs. Charles F. Suttle and William Brent, "for, that the said Suttle and Brent, on the 24th day of May instant, well knowing the said Burns to be a free citizen of Massachusetts, conspired together to have the said Burns arrested and imprisoned as a slave of said Suttle, and carried to Alexandria, Va.," &c., &c. — Lewis Hayden, a colored man, was the complainant in the case. The writ was served upon Messrs. Suttle and Brent, and they gave the required bail in the sum of $5,000 each. Subsequently, Chief Justice Wells issued a writ of replevin against United States Marshal Freeman, directing that officer to bring the body of Anthony Burns, the fugitive, before the Court of Common Pleas, on the 7th day of June next, but the Marshal did not obey the order.

HOW BURNS WAS DISCOVERED.

Soon after Burns' arrival here, as it now appears, he wrote a letter to his brother in Alexandria, who is also a slave of Mr. Suttle's, stating that he was at work with Coffin Pitts, in Brattle street, cleaning old clothes. This letter he dated in "Boston," but sent it to Canada, where it was postmarked and sent according to the superscription, to Burns' brother in Alexandria. As is the custom at the South, when letters are received directed to slaves they are delivered to the owner of such slaves, who opens them and examines their contents. This appears to have been the case with Burns' letter, and by his own hand his place of retreat was discovered by his master.

THE ARRAIGNMENT OF THE RIOTERS.

The prisoners arrested Friday evening, consisting of Albert J. Brown, Jr., (law student) of Cambridge; John J. Roberts, Walter Phœnix, (colored); John Wesley, (colored); Walter Bishop, (colored); Thomas Jackson, (colored); Henry Howe, Martin Stowell, of Worcester, John Thompson, were examined this afternoon in the Police Court, Judge Rogers, presiding.

The complaint was made by Deputy Chief Luther A. Ham, and charges the whole number, collectively, with having committed, with malice aforethought, a felonious assault, on the 26th day of May, 1854, upon the person of James Batchelder, with firearms loaded with powder and ball, and that they did kill and murder the said Batchelder. Mr. Ham proposed to the Court that, as the Government were not prepared to enter upon the case, the examination of the prisoners be postponed until Wednesday next. Charles G. Davis, Esq., counsel for the prisoners, objected to the complaint, on the ground that it appeared that the charge of murder (not being bailable) was preferred against the whole number, merely to hold them all over, it being the last day in the week. He wished to inquire if some of the prisoners were not arrested before the homicide took place; and, if so, he held that they should be admitted to bail.

The Judge postponed the hearing of the cases until Tuesday next, and they were committed to jail.

George Palmer, one of the persons arrested in Court Square, this forenoon, has been committed to jail, charged with assaulting an officer. Nichols, Smith, Thayer, and Jewell, were discharged.

INCIDENTS OF THE AFTERNOON AND NIGHT.

Great excitement has prevailed this (Saturday) evening, and during the afternoon. Thousands of curious persons have been attracted to the Court House, and several arrests of disorderly persons have been made.

While W. C. Fay, Esq., was conversing with another person, his remarks excited the ire of a stalwart negro, named Wilson Hopewell, who struck Mr. Fay. Officer William B. Tarleton arrested him, when a violent struggle ensued. Hopewell drew a dirk knife, but before he had opportunity to use it, the officer wrested it from his grasp, and succeeded in conveying him to the Centre Watch House, and subsequently to jail. During the scuffle the officer had his hat demolished and his coat torn off. The man seized Mr. Tarleton by the throat, not releasing his grasp till he had reached the Watch House.

Two drunken persons were taken from the crowd, and locked up.

Miss Hinkley, a well dressed woman, tried more than two hours to force her way into the Court House. Officer J. C. Warren declared this the most remarkable case of feminine curiosity which has ever occurred under his practice.

A man from Worcester, whose name was unknown, took his position on an inverted flour barrel, and harangued the crowd for a few minutes, on Abolitionism and Bill Nebraska; but, before he had closed, an officer assisted him to the watch house.

John C. Cluer was arrested this afternoon, on the charge of riotous proceedings, and is now in jail.

We learn this evening that a post mortem examination of Batchelder was made to day, and it was ascertained that he was not shot, but was stabbed, the wound being six inches deep. When he fell, he exclaimed, "I am stabbed."

The precept for calling out the Boston companies was placed in the hands of Major General B. F. Edmands, this morning, and the Boston Light Infantry and Cadets were called out, to PRESERVE ORDER AND KEEP THE PEACE. The troops of this State have nothing to do with the safety of Burns, who is so well guarded that no mob could enter the court house and rescue him. The Cadets remained on duty all night, and the Boston Light Infantry were relieved by the New England Guards, Capt. Henshaw.

The prisoner is a stout, good-looking negro, and appears much dejected, though by no means morose or disposed to obstinacy.

It is understood that the claimant will sell Burns here in Boston, for a reasonable sum; and yesterday afternoon some peaceably disposed persons seemed on the point of raising a contribution for the purpose of the purchase.

There were many rumors afloat during the afternoon, among which was the statement that a large number of persons had arrived in town — parties who would manifest the strongest opposition to having Burns returned to Virginia. It was also reported that 400 colored persons, from New Bedford, had arrived in the city.

Col. Suttle, the claimant of Burns, and Mr. Brent, the witness, are gentlemen of high social position and men of wealth. They come on here to test the law, in a fair and honorable way, and they ask for simple justice.

It is stated that the United States authorities at Washington have telegraphed to the United States Marshal here to have the law carried out, and to call the United States troops here, and even those at more distant stations, to their aid for that purpose.

The leading Free Soilers in this city deprecate, in the strongest terms, the course pursued by the mob last night. We heard one observe to-day, who had been a leader in their ranks, that, by their conduct, they condemned Burns to slavery.

Thousands of false rumors are in circulation to-day relating to Burns, and what has been said and threatened. We have no room to give such falsehoods currency.

The wife of Batchelder knew nothing of his death until this morning, when the announcement was made to her by a lady, who saw the account of the occurrence in the morning papers. She chanced to be in the front yard, and immediately fainted, and was taken into the house. He leaves no children.

About half past seven o'clock, last evening, the Cadets, Colonel Amory, were drawn up into line in Court Square, and Mayor Smith being introduced to the company, made a brief and very appropriate speech, expressing his confidence in their efficiency and honesty of purpose, and remarked the orderly spirit generally manifested by the citizens.

At eight o'clock, Chief of Police Taylor, with a force of police, cleared Court Square, and stretched ropes across the avenue leading to it, so as to render ingress impossible without great force.

It was rumored that the Truckmen intended to make a "demonstration" for the especial benefit of Wendell Phillips, Esq., Wm. L. Garrison, Rev. Theodore Parker, and Swift, and so general was the rumor, and so currently believed, that numerous applications were made to the Mayor to protect the persons and property of people in the vicinity of those houses.

During this evening a number of men were seen to approach the dwellings of Messrs. Phillips and Parker, and to read the name and number carefully, and then to proceed; but up to twelve o'clock there had been no violent demonstration. The Mayor had taken every precaution, having runners or couriers out in every direction, who could furnish reliable information from any point in the city in less than five minutes. Capt. W. D. Eaton, with thirty-four of the best men in the department, were in readiness to be called into service at a moment's warning, and other men; a large force were concealed and also ready for action. Suspicious persons were closely watched, but no violence was attempted. Among the applicants to the Mayor for protection of Mr. Phillips was a man from South Reading, who seemed much interested in the city's affairs.

At eleven o'clock it was confidently stated that Burns would be purchased by Wendell Phillips and Francis Jackson, for $1200. Sufficient money was raised early in the evening, but it was supposed that there was some flaw in some one of the legal documents, which might afford a loop-hole large enough for him to crawl out at, and thus save the compromise.

At nine o'clock the New England Guards, forty-nine guns, Capt. Henshaw. came on duty, and quartered at City Hall. It was stated that the Light Guard were in their armory. The Cadets were quartered at the Albion. Sergeants' Guards of the Light Dragoons and Lancers were at their armories. Orders were given that, in case of any outbreak, the military should report to Gen. Edmands and Col. Amory.

The Mayor remained at the police office all night, as that was the nearest point of information. He has had a trying time. It was said that, during the day, not less than *one thousand* pistols, principally revolvers, were bought in Dock Square and vicinity.

Officers Tarlton and Cheswell found upon the negro Hopewell, who was arrested at 6 1-2 o'clock, a large African knife, called a *creece* — just such a knife as must have been used to inflict the death wound of poor Batchelder. A charge of murder will be preferred against him to-day.

The excitement was intense, but no violence or loud cries were made in or about the Court House.

A gentleman stated at the police office that a Worcester man was heard to say that 200 people had come from Worcester, and would not return "till the thing had been settled."

The mob gathered in front of the court house this evening, threw several stones, bricks, &c., with a view of breaking the windows in the building. One of the stones struck a member of the New England Guards, while on duty.

The following persons were arrested this evening, about 10 1-2 o'clock, for riotous conduct in front of the court house : James Bellows, (on whose person was a dirk knife,) Lewis Osgood, Thomas Faritan, Charles H. Crichnay, Joseph Brown, and James Cunningham. They were taken to the centre watch house, and subsequently to jail. Examination on Monday.

General Edmands and his staff established their headquarters at the Albion. where they have been in attendance during the day.

At midnight, some two hundred persons were around the court house, consisting chiefly of the curious, many colored persons, and about twenty colored females.

Great credit is due to the police, for the manner in which they have managed matters to-day. Mr. Taylor has been untiring in his efforts, and his coolness and courage on Friday evening were very evidently and successfully shown.

Sunday Morning, May 28, 2 o'clock.

BURNS TO BE LIBERATED.

The negotiations for the purchase of the alleged fugitive slave Burns were well nigh consummated last night, and the proceedings were carried so far as to leave little doubt. Burns will be bought and liberated either to-day, or at the close of the examination before the United States Commissioner. The following is a copy of a document which was drawn up in the office of Edward G. Loring, Esq., last night, and signed by several prominent merchants and colored men : —

"BOSTON, May 27th, 1854.

"We, the undersigned, agree to pay Anthony Burns, or order, the sum set against our respective names, for the purpose of enabling him to obtain his freedom from the United States Government, in the hands of whose officers he is now held as a slave."

This paper will be presented by the Rev. L. A. Grimes, pastor of the Twelfth Baptist Church.

The sum of $1200 — the amount specified by the owner as the price of the man — was made up by colored persons, a part being given on condition that the bargain be consummated last night, but this was found to be impossible, on account of the lateness of the hour. The counsel on both sides, as also District Attorney Hallett, were present in the United States Marshal's room, and all acquiesced in the arrangement. It will be the more satisfactory to the friends of Burns to let the examination proceed, and the ownership of the man clearly proved, as the title will be all the stronger. The money has been raised, the owner is willing to sell the man, and the papers are nearly ready for signing. It was hoped that the bargain would have been consummated last night; and so confident were certain parties of it, that Mr. Grimes was present, the money in *specie* was ready. A carriage was at the door, and several merchants stood ready to see the man delivered. It is now only a matter of time, and the excitement will, therefore, at once be abated. He will be detained in the court house till Monday. The crowd of persons remained in Court street till an early hour this morning.

The following from the Commonwealth.

ANOTHER MAN SEIZED IN BOSTON

— BY THE —

MAN HUNTERS!!

THE DEVIL-BILL RENEWING ITS VIGOR

AND GETTING UP A JUBILEE AMONG US,

ON THE PASSAGE OF THE

NEBRASKA BILL!!!

Another colored man was seized in this city Wednesday night by virtue of that devil's license for kidnapping, the Fugitive Slave Bill, and was at the Court House, before the Fugitive Slave Bill Commissioner, Thursday morning. The hunt was conducted so stealthily that few, if any but those directly concerned in it, knew any thing of the matter until the man was seized and taken before the commissioner. The news presently began to circulate about the city, and people were just beginning to gather at the Court House when the examination was adjourned to Saturday. The proceedings before the commissioner furnished the following particulars.—

The colored man was taken Wednesday night in Court Square, between six and seven o'clock, and kept in durance all night in the Court House. Yesterday morning about nine o'clock he was brought before Commissioner Edward G. Loring for examination. E. G. Parker, Esq., appeared in behalf of the man-hunters, and used documents purporting to be from the circuit court of the county of Alexandria, in Virginia, which set forth that Charles F. Suttle, of Alexandria, in that State, is the owner of a certain colored man named Anthony Burns. The documents describe this Burns as a man about six feet high, twenty-four years old, and refer particularly to "scars" on his cheek and hand. It was alleged, in substance, that the man under arrest is this Burns, that he ran away from his owner some time in March last, and that the hunters mean to take this man to Virginia, there to be held and treated as a chattel.

William Brent was sworn and testified: I am a merchant residing in Richmond; know Charles F. Suttle; he is a merchant; know the boy Anthony Burns; the prisoner is said Burns; he is Suttle's slave; he was born in Suttle's family; I hired him of Suttle in 1847–'48–'49; I know he was missing from Richmond about the 24th of March last; have not seen him there since; have had no conversation with him here.

R. H. Dana, Jr., here rose and said, —

May it please your honor — I rise to address the court as *amicus curiæ*, for I cannot say that I am regularly of counsel for the person at the bar. Indeed, from the few words I have been enabled to hold with him, and from what I can learn from others who have talked with him, I am satisfied he is not in a condition to determine whether he will have counsel or not, or whether or not, and how, he shall prepare for his defence. He declines to say whether any one shall appear for him, or whether he will defend or not.

Under these circumstances I submit to your honor's judgment that time should be allowed to the prisoner to recover himself from the stupefaction of his sudden arrest and his novel and distressing situation, and have opportunity to consult with friends and members of the bar, and determine what course he will pursue.

E. G. Parker, Esq., for the claimant. I feel bound to oppose the motion. The counsel himself says that the prisoner does not wish for counsel and does not wish for a defence. The only object of a delay is to try to induce him to resist the just claim which he is now ready to acknowledge. The delay will cause great inconvenience to my client, the claimant, and his witness, both of whom have come all the way from Virginia for this purpose, and will be delayed here a day or two if this adjournment is granted. If it were suggested that the prisoner was insane — out of his mind — and would be likely to recover soon, we could not object. As it is, we do object.

To this Mr. Dana replied: The counsel for the prosecution misapprehends my statement. I did not say that the prisoner did not wish counsel and defence. I said that he was evidently not in a state to say what he wishes to do. Indeed, he has said that he is willing to have a trial; but I am not willing to act on such a statement as that. He does not know what he is saying. I say to your honor, as a member of the bar, on my personal responsibility, that from what I have seen of the man and from what I have learned from others who have seen him, that he is not in a fit state to decide for himself what he will do. He has just been arrested and brought into this scene, with this immense stake of freedom or slavery for life at issue, surrounded by strangers; and, even if he should plead guilty to the claim, the court ought not to receive the plea under such circumstances. It is but yesterday that the court at the other end of this building refused a plea of guilty from a prisoner. The court never will receive this plea in a capital case without the fullest proof that the prisoner makes it deliberately and understands its meaning and his own situation, and has consulted with friends. In a case involving freedom or slavery for life, this court will not do less.

The counsel for the claimant objects to a delay; he objects on the ground of the inconvenience to which it will put the claimant and his witness, who have come all the way from Virginia for this purpose. I can assure him, I think, that he mistakes the character of this tribunal by addressing to it such an argument as that. We have not yet come to that state in which we cannot weigh liberty against convenience, and freedom against pecuniary expense. We have yet something left by which we can measure those qualities.

I know enough of this tribunal to know that it will not lend itself to the hurrying of a man into slavery, to accommodate any man's personal convenience, before he has even time to recover his stupefied faculties, and say whether he has a defence or not. Even without a suggestion from an *amicus curiæ* the court would, of its own motion, see to it that no such advantage was taken.

The counsel for the claimant says that if the man were out of his mind he would not object. Out of his mind! Please your honor, if you had ever reason to fear that a prisoner was not in full possession of his mind, you would fear it in such a case as this. But I have said enough. I am confident your honor will not decide so momentous an issue against a man without counsel and without opportunity.

C. M. Ellis, Esq., also argued in favor of postponement. He stated that a decision in so important a case, should not be given, until the fullest and fairest trial, and this they had a right to demand. There could be no fear of delay, with the power of the United States and Massachusetts to sustain the authorities; the only fear is, that justice may not be done. The prisoner had the right to have all the allegations made against him proved, and also to be provided with counsel to advise him and conduct his defence. There is also a necessity, he said, for delay, in order that the friends of the prisoner may deliberate as to the course they shall pursue. In conclusion, he argued that justice, meagre as it is under this law, should be meted out; but there should be no violence, no court house in chains, but a full and fair investigation of the case.

The Commissioner then addressed the prisoner, who seemed frightened at his position, and informed him it was his right to have all the allegations made against him proved by the clearest testimony; that he had also the right to have counsel and friends, and that if he desired a postponement, he should accord it to him. The prisoner seemed in great doubt what to say. He glanced around the court house, apparently in search of some one. After a few moments delay, he, in a low voice, asked to have the case postponed. Accordingly Commissioner Loring postponed the further examination of the case to Saturday next, at nine o'clock, A. M. Meanwhile the man will be kept imprisoned in the court room.

There will be a meeting of the people in Faneuil Hall, this evening, to consider this matter. We have one word for our city officers. Let them read the Statutes of the Commonwealth, and consider well what they are about, before they allow themselves to be engaged in the service of these man hunters. It is just possible, that our city authorities will not again trample under foot the laws of the State, in the service of the fugitive slave bill, without being held responsible for it.

This man, whom Suttle claims as his slave, came to Boston about three weeks ago, and has been at work for Coffin Pitts, in Brattle street. Wednesday night, after he had put up the shutters and closed the shop, he went away in the direction of Court street. He was immediately followed by the man hunters, who had been lying in wait for him, under the orders of Watson Freeman, Pierce's United States Marshal. He was taken into custody by officers Coolidge, Riley, and Leighton. He made no resistance. They took him to the court house, where he was kept all night under a strong guard. He seemed stunned and stupefied by fear. The news of the arrest did not get abroad, and his valiant keepers did not deem it necessary to get out the old chain and stretch it round the court house.

During the evening, Suttle was permitted to see and converse with him. This did not restore the poor fellow's equanimity and self-possession, especially when the slaveholder told him he must go with him to Virginia. Suttle told him to "make no noise about it," and go quietly, and he "shouldn't be hurt." He represents that the prisoner professed a willingness to go; but the public can easily appreciate this talk of "willingness" to be carried off as a chattel, in such a man, suddenly seized by the fugitive slave bill's bloodhounds, and stupefied with fear, of the doom to which they attempt to drag him. Under such appliances, he is not likely to give a very clear account of what he is willing to do. So far as he understood what was said to him, he probably construed it this: " You *must* go with me as my slave; make no noise, go quietly, seem willing to go, and I will not harm you; but refuse to go, and resist my purpose to take you away, and I will flog you horribly." Is it difficult to comprehend why he hardly dared Thursday morning, to admit to the Commissioner that he desired a postponement of the examination?

" Shall Boston steal another man?" That is the question now before us. The federal Constitution was framed to "establish justice" and "secure the blessings of liberty," not to patronize the scoundrelisms of slavery. If it were otherwise, if the instrument were so atrocious, so false to the Declaration of Independence, as to give one man a right to enslave another and make him his property, his chattel, it would still remain true, that it provides that the "trial of all crimes, except in cases of impeachment, shall be by jury," and that "in suits at common law, where the value in controversy shall exceed twenty dollars, the right of trial by jury shall be preserved."

In defiance and scorn of these great principles of the Constitution, these creatures of slavery come here armed with that infernal machine for kidnapping, the unconstitutional and most atrocious fugitive slave bill, and mean to deny this man's right to freedom, and subject him to slavery for life, without allowing him trial by jury, or admitting that freedom can have a right to make its claims heard of in presence of the slave power. They seized him in the streets of our city, and in scorn of the great principles of the Constitution, and defiance of that due process of law which it says "shall be preserved," they mean to bear him off in triumph and plunge him into the hell of slavery. Then will these slaveholders again laugh us to scorn, sneer at us as "mean, sneaking, degenerate, pliant, huckstering, peddling Greeks," and boast that they will soon have a law authorizing them to hold slaves on Bunker Hill. " Shall Boston steal another man?"

FANEUIL HALL TO-NIGHT.

For the third time, Boston witnesses the disgraceful spectacle of a man charged with not the shadow of crime — accused of nothing but obedience to the upward yearnings of a spirit that bade him reach the same inalienable right to life, liberty, and the pursuit of happiness which we enjoy, and which the accursed statutes of Virginia denied him — chained like a felon, in a Boston court house, thus thrice degraded to a jail! — awaiting the mockery of a trial which shall doom him to all the unutterable misery, horror, and blackness of darkness faintly shadowed beneath that word — SLAVERY! — without once allowing him to look upon the face of a judge — the faces of a jury; — without giving him one chance for a future way of life far more precious than life itself, by securing to him the smallest of those privileges of justice, won for him, as for us all, by the best blood of " exile and ancestor!"

To-night — thank God! — we meet in Faneuil Hall, without distinction of party, to consider our duty in the premises. Let there be a meeting of men who are thoroughly and religiously in earnest, and who are willing to do and help do, every noble thing in their power, to save the living soul and body of a fellow man from the blistering and withering hell of southern slavery! Let every man who reads these words remember that this is indeed one of the crises of liberty, and let him look to it that he be not absent to-night from Faneuil Hall! The slave power crams the infamous swindle of a Nebraska bill down our throats, and then piles an outrage upon an insult, and undertakes to steal a MAN! Leave your fields, your work-shops, your stores, your homes — leave every occupation, duty, and pleasure, and swarm to Boston! Let no man who loves liberty for himself or another, and who has five dollars in his pocket, stay away! Northern yeomen and mechanics, and tradesmen of every order, and degree! you owe to the genius of your Massachusetts liberty the solemn duty of your presence — you owe to her your stern, indignant protest against this monstrous and atrocious wrong — if you owe nothing more!

WHO ARE THEY?

It is surmised that the men who are guarding Burns, at the court house, are the identical ones who passed the resolves in the Democratic County Convention, in favor of the extension of slavery into Nebraska, and fired guns on the Common in honor of such extension. They are probably paid by the custom house. Let not the *city* have a hand in this business.

Boston court house stands among us as the Bastile of the slave power — entirely at the service of that malign despotism, whenever it comes among us with its kidnapping bill, to hunt down men whose only crime is an ardent longing to enjoy that freedom to which every man has an "inalienable right." It stirs one's blood with shame and indignation to know this. When the slaveholders get their law for holding slaves on Bunker Hill, probably the monument will be their Bastile, with the black flag floating over it, bearing the inscription, — "Slavery is King — there is no higher law." And there will be "peace and quiet" in the land when this hideous and bloody despot has "crushed out" all who have manhood enough to question his right to reign.

THE GARRISONED SLAVE PEN.

One of the papers stated that Boston court house, Saturday morning, resembled a "beleaguered fortress." It should have said "Bastile," or "fortified slave pen." Some of the windows on the west side were broken, and the southwesterly door showed abundant signs of the fierce contest that took place there the night previous. To our readers at a distance it may be interesting to give some description of this building. It is a large oblong structure, strongly built of hewn blocks of granite. It is four stories high above the basement, and the interior consists of rooms, stairways, and narrow passages. Its north end fronts on Court street, from which there are wide spaces on each side of it. Just south of the court house is the City Hall, which fronts southerly on School street, with a well kept yard before it.

The United States District Court has been permitted to hold its sessions in a room in the second story of the court house, and by virtue of this permission the government officials assume or take authority to use the building as a prison and fortress of the slave power. We commend this fact to the sober attention of people of Massachusetts. Does not a law of this State provide that our public buildings shall not be used as jails by the officials of the general government? And are not our local authorities bound to execute this law?

Saturday, May 27th.

The examination of Burns was resumed in the United States District Court Room, before Commissioner Loring, this morning, at 10 o'clock. At nine o'clock, Burns was brought into the court room from the upper room, where he had been confined, accompanied by a strong guard, and handcuffed. He looked dejected and anxious. The passage way to the court room was strongly guarded, and within the room was a strong force of armed men surrounding the prisoner.

Seth J. Thomas, Esq., and Edward G. Parker, Esq., appeared as counsel for the claimants, and Richard H. Dana, Jr., and Charles M. Ellis, Esqs., for the fugitive.

Mr. Ellis asked for a further delay, for the purpose of preparing the case on the part of the fugitive. We were not counsel for the prisoner at the former hearing, but only interposed to secure public justice, and so that the proceedings might secure public respect. He said that it was not till yesterday afternoon that Mr. Dana or himself felt at liberty to act for the prisoner. He understood that all persons except Mr. Dana were prohibited from access to the prisoner, and he did not feel at liberty, after what had transpired here, to approach him and volunteer his counsel.

They did not volunteer as his counsel on the first hearing. Yesterday afternoon, for the first time, had we any right to prepare a defence. It therefore stands as if this person was seized yesterday afternoon, and was brought in here this morning for examination. Is it fit that this case should be tried under these circumstances? He had never spoken to the fugitive. They therefore ask that a reasonable delay might be granted. It is fitting there should be a delay, under the circumstances by which we are surrounded. He had not supposed this thing would ever happen here again — that a man would be sure of a full, free, and fair trial; but it is not so. This case does not come up as the cases three or four years ago. It was then put to people here that we should acquiesce; the law could be enforced, and we should have no more of it. But it is not so now. The man stands here as a freeman, entitled to all the protection the laws can throw around him. He asked his honor to consider that this was the only tribunal between the man and perpetual slavery. He feared it was to be settled here that there was no process which could interfere here. He reminded the Commissioner that he acted as judge and jury in this case, and he ought to be able to say that he had given every chance for preparation, for reflection. If you must approach this case, I beg you to pause and give him time for preparation, and until you can approach it without bias, which the counsel said he could not. He urged the excitement of the morning as a peculiar reason why the request of delay should be granted.

He desired to say that he had no personal invitation to attend the meeting last evening, and had no inclination to do it. He thought there was force enough to have this trial go on in the ordinary way. He thought there was fault in the show of force, for that begets force.

Mr. Parker objected to a further continuance of the case. When the case first came on, the learned counsel said the fugitive was not in a state of mind to determine whether he would have counsel to cross-question the witness. On such a plea he did not object to delay; and delay was granted on that ground. Now it is not pretended that he is in that state of mind, but they have not had time to prepare the case. The argument is, that the proceedings here are to settle the case of the man's freedom or slavery. This is not so, but is only a preliminary hearing, to determine the question of sending the man to a place where the question of his condition will be settled, according to the laws which are presumed to exist there. He therefore saw no reason for delay. In the excited condition of the public mind, it is best that the matter should be disposed of as speedily as is consistent with justice.

Mr. Thomas asked his Honor to consider the nature of the case; the petition for delay, and the ground for opposing the petition. He referred to the other hearing, and said that those who appeared for the fugitive then did not say that they had any defence to make. He admitted that at that hearing the fugitive was not in a proper state of mind to go on. The fugitive then admitted that he had no defence to make, and only wanted time to think what to do. The case is this: if the claimant has property in this man, and it is proved, the only duty of your Honor is to grant a certificate for his removal to a place where the case is to be decided.

What cause, he asked, is shown for continuance? They say that they have not had time to prepare for the defence. The plea that his counsel had not been permitted to see him was, not correct. The Marshal sent word to Mr. Dana that he might have access to him. He thought the counsel for the man knew that they had not any substantial ground of defence. It was not suggested that they could bring evidence to disprove the facts of the ownership of the claimant in this man. He did not see any thing which could be presented in matter of fact for delay, and therefore he saw no reason for granting the delay.

He alluded to the results of the delay the other day, the excitement last night, and those engaged in it; and said, if they could lay their heads on their pillows and not feel that the blood of a fellow man rests upon their heads, he should be glad to know it. From this excitement he drew an argument for the prompt settlement of this case.

The learned counsel stated at length the nature of the case, and the provisions made by the United States laws for the reclamation of fugitives. This case, he said, was similar to one where a man has a promissory note against another and proceeded under the law to get it. The objection, he said, is not to the facts in the case, but it is to giving him up in conformity to the law. They don't like the law, but it is nevertheless a law, and is binding on the courts. Since he has no defence, since it is not suggested that they wish to get evidence and change the nature of the case, what is the reason for the continuance? He did not believe the man would be in as calm a state of mind on Monday as he is to-day, under the excitement which exists about him. It is in effect an attempt to render this law invalid. It is no less treason to defeat the operation of this law than it would be to go to the other end of the court house and rescue a man convicted for murder. The law has been pronounced constitutional by our Supreme Court, and by other high judicial bodies, and he saw no objection brought up here which is not against the law and not against the facts.

Mr. Dana, for the fugitive, understood the simple question to be, whether he shall be hurried into a trial now, or shall have reasonable time to prepare for it. He cited the Simms case, in which seven days delay was granted, and said we have not asked half that time. He stated the facts of the arrest of Burns, at night, under a false pretence, and his being hurried to the court house, which has not been kept as a jail, but as a slave pen. The next morning, at nine o'clock, he was hurried in here, and, up to that time, he had seen no one. I was going past the court house, and heard there was a fugitive here, and came in voluntarily, and found the proceedings beginning, and offered him my services. I found him stupefied, and acting under terror. I believed that the reason which governed, Burns was, that if he put the claimant to any delay he would suffer for it. Burns said I might defend him if I chose. I did not wish to take the responsibility under the circumstances. Mr. Dana rehearsed the questioning of Burns by the court, and the delay granted at his request. Burns was then left without counsel. An order was passed to admit me on Thursday to see him; but I was not willing to see him under the circumstances. He had not made up his mind that he wished to make a defence, and I had no right as a member of this bar to go to him until I had a request from him to act as his counsel. The next thing was to get some persons who should go and see him, and Mr. Grimes, the colored clergyman, and Deacon Pitts, were selected.

They asked the Marshal for leave to visit him, and it was refused. He was told that the Marshal would not admit these friends even if the Commissioner requested it. An order was procured, however, about noon yesterday, and the Marshal admitted them. It is less than twenty-four hours since that man was permitted to see him, and make known his wishes in regard to counsel. About 2 o'clock yesterday, his friends called on me and said he wanted to make a defence, and asked me to appear as his counsel. Mr. Ellis was engaged about the same time. If he stopped there he should have a good ground for delay — but he would go further.

The first thing done by his counsel, was to try to relieve this court of this case, and an effort was made to get a writ of *de homine replegiando* from Judge Sprague, and at six o'clock it was refused. He did not believe the court would hear the argument of the counsel on the other side, that if the case was delayed there would be disturbance. That is an argument that can be addressed to no court, for it is a confession of weakness — that the law is not strong, and therefore the man must suffer.

Mr. Dana then reviewed the nature of the record, which was put in as proof in this case, and which he had had a copy of only since last evening, and argued that the granting of the certificate settled the case of Burns finally; that he would never go before another tribunal, but might, and Burns himself feared that he would, be sold to go to New Orleans.

The claimant might send him where he pleases, and your Honor could not help it. If the case goes on now he will say, and we shall say, he has not had a defence. It is in view of the tremendous consequences of granting this certificate that they asked delay.

In conclusion, he repeated his request for delay.

In reply to the suggestion that Burns might be sold at the first slave mart, Mr. Parker said that the claimant had consented to selling him here.

The Commissioner then gave his decision in the case. He said there was a difference in granting a delay in proceedings before this court in a hearing of this kind, from the delays before other courts, where delays are made for periods of weeks or months, and where important testimony may be lost by the death of witnesses, or by other causes. He looked upon Burns as one who is yet to be regarded as a freeman; he knew of no proof yet submitted that he was to be regarded as any thing else. He was arrested on Wednesday night, and on Thursday morning, at the hearing, expressed a desire for delay, that he might make up his mind what course he should pursue. The delay was granted, and he had improved it by obtaining counsel. Now his counsel being chosen by him, come into court and say that they are not prepared to go on with this case, and they cannot go on now and do their client justice. The question of delay is one within the discretion of the court to grant. He thought the request was a reasonable one. As to the excitement in the community, he regretted it, but he could not consider it in this case. He must look at the rights of the parties, and see that justice is done. It seems that one or two days' delay is not an unreasonable request, and I therefore grant further delay until Monday morning, at 11 o'clock.

Upon the rendering of the decision, the crowd which had thronged the court room quietly left, and Burns was taken to his quarters in the upper story of the building — all the avenues to which are protected by United States troops. On each landing of the stairs there is a squad of marines and United States troops posted with fixed bayonets, and there are numbers of troops in the rooms of each story. Probably five thousand men could not force an entrance to the second story of the building, so strongly is it guarded.

Large ropes, instead of chains, are now employed to fence out the people from the passages down the sides of the Court House; and these rope barricades are guarded by the *Boston Police!!* The Court House itself is garrisoned by United States troops, some of whom were quartered in the fourth story and others in the second story, where Saturday and Sunday they were seen lounging about the windows, and gazing at the crowd in Court street. The poor fellow against whose liberty this force is marshalled, could now and then be seen on Sunday, looking from a third story window on the west side, in the room where he is held by the Marshal and his aids. Such is one picture of man-hunting in Boston.

The military of the city which has been called out by the Mayor, was quartered in the City Hall, where they could be seen from the windows yesterday. The documents will explain how they were called into this service:

COMMONWEALTH OF MASSACHUSETTS.

SUFFOLK, ss.   BOSTON, May 26th, 1854.

To Col. Robert Cowdin, commanding the Fifth Regiment of Artillery of Massachusetts Volunteer Militia.

Whereas, it has been made to appear to me, J. V. C. Smith, Mayor of Boston, that there is threatened a tumult, riot and mob of a body of men, acting together by force with intent to offer violence to persons and property, and by force and violence to break and resist the laws of this Commonwealth, in the said County of Suffolk, and that Military Force is necessary to aid the civil authorities in suppressing the same.

Now therefore, I command you, that you cause two companies of Artillery, armed and equipped, and with ammunition as the law directs, and with proper officers attached, to be detailed by you to parade at said Boston, on this evening, at their respective armories, then and there to obey such orders as may be given them according to law. Hereof fail not at your peril, and have you there then this warrant with your doings returned thereon. Witness my hand and the seal of the City of Boston, this twenty-sixth day of May, 1854.

                                              J. V. C. SMITH,
                                              Mayor of the City of Boston.

Immediately upon the reception of the above document, Col. Cowdin issued the following order:—

                    Head Quarters, 5th Reg. Art., 1st Brig., 2d }
                        Div. M. V. M., Boston, May 26, 1854.   }

In obedience to a requisition from his Honor, J. V. C. Smith, Mayor of Boston the Captains commanding Companies A and B, of this regiment, will report with the companies under their command, at City Hall, forthwith, uniformed, armed, and equipped as the law directs for special duty, and there await further orders.

                    Signed,   ROBERT COWDIN, Col.

Capts. of Companies A and B.

                    Head Quarters 5th Reg., 1st Brig., 1st Div. }
                        M. V. M., Boston, May 27, 1854.   }

In obedience to Division and Brigade orders of this date, the commanders of companies composing this Regiment, will cause a detail of four privates, under command of a corporal, to assemble at their Armory, uniformed, armed, and equipped as the law directs, for special guard duty, and there wait further orders. Per order,

                                              ROBERT COWDIN, Col.

F. A. HEATH, Adjt.

Subsequently the Mayor issued his precept, similar to the one received by Col. Cowdin, to Maj. Gen. Edmands, and the Independent Cadets and Boston Light Infantry were detailed for duty of the same kind.

It will be noticed that they are called out to suppress " tumult, riot, and mob," by those who intend " to break and resist the laws of this Commonwealth," and that they are " to obey such orders as may be given them according to law." We should like to know what law of this Commonwealth authorizes or *permits* the Boston police to serve as sentries for the garrison in that fortified slave pen, commonly called " Boston Court House." But here is a brave array of troops, marshals, police, and enlisted creatures of various sorts, — all on duty to crush out the freedom of a poor fellow, whose only crime is a decided repugnance to slavery. The Sunday *Despatch* had the following : —

" It may be a matter of interest to the riotously disposed to know that a force of 10,000 men could not rescue Burns. Every avenue in the Court House bristles with bayonets, and should an attack be made, the air would whirl with bullets. Those who desire one of the sort, had better try a little of the rescue game.
A despatch was received in this city, Saturday, from Washington, by the United States Marshal, directing him to have the fugitive slave trial carried through as promptly as possible, and the law executed to the letter. Also authorizing him to call upon all the United States troops in the vicinity for assistance, and if needed, to send to New York for reinforcements. The Marshal responded that it SHOULD BE DONE ! "

" Send to New York for reinforcements ! " The whole army and navy will probably be employed to get hold of this man and get him out of Boston. We met some Germans yesterday, who had been taking a look at the Court House. They were much excited by what they saw, and one of them, pointing to the soldiers, said " and you call this a free country ! " One element of the excitement, Saturday evening, is reported by the *Gazette*, as follows : —

It was rumored that the truckmen intended to make a " demonstration " for the especial benefit of Wendell Phillips, William Lloyd Garrison, Rev. Theodore Parker, and Swift, and so general was the rumor and so currently believed, that numerous applications were made to the Mayor to protect the persons and property of people in the vicinity of those houses. During this evening a number of men were seen to approach the dwellings of Messrs. Phillips and Parker and to read the name and number carefully, and then to proceed; but up to 12 o'clock there had been no violent demonstration. The Mayor had taken every precaution, having runners or couriers out in every direction who could furnish reliable information from any point in the city in less than five minutes. Capt. W. D. Eaton, with 34 of the best men in the department were in readiness to be called into service at a moment's warning, and other men, — a large force were concealed and also ready for action. Suspicious persons were closely watched but no violence was attempted.

SUTTLE REFUSES TO SELL BURNS.

Mr. Parker, Suttle's counsel, stated before the commissioner, Saturday, that he was willing to sell Burns for his fair market value as a slave. Endeavors were accordingly made to rescue the man by paying the claimant's price for him. Suttle agreed to give him up for twelve hundred dollars. This sum was raised immediately; but then he averred that he must also have all the expenses paid ; and finally said that he was counselled not to give the man up at any rate. We hear that the commissioner advised him to conclude the arrangement for the sale that had been agreed on, and that Mr. Hallett used his influence to prevent it, and also that Suttle has received a despatch from Virginia, urging him to take the man back at any rate. The gentlemen who sought to buy off the claimant were in consultation on the subject until midnight, Saturday. When the result was known the following handbill was put in circulation : —

"THE MAN IS NOT BOUGHT!

HE IS STILL IN THE SLAVE PEN IN THE COURT HOUSE.

The kidnapper agreed, both publicly and in writing, to sell him for twelve hundred dollars. The sum was raised by eminent Boston citizens, and offered him. He then claimed more. The bargain was broken. The kidnapper breaks his agreement, though even the United States commissioner advised him to keep it. *Be on your guard against all lies.* WATCH THE SLAVE PEN. Let every man attend the trial. Remember Monday morning at 11 o'clock."

We stated, Saturday, that this man hunt in Boston was deliberately contrived and intended as an outrage to the principles and feelings of men in the free states, to be perpetrated by way of jubilee over the passage of the Nebraska Bill. This was said at one of our hotels, Friday evening, by a gentleman from Northern Virginia, and was told to us by the gentleman to whom he said it, and whom he seems to have mistaken for a southerner. The final refusal to sell the man plainly confirms this statement.

SERVICES AT THE MUSIC HALL.

There was an immense audience at the Music Hall yesterday to hear Rev Theodore Parker. There was a general expectation that he would have a " Lesson for the Day," and that vast hall, with its double tier of galleries, could not contain all the people who sought admittance. Mr. Parker delivered a short extempore discourse on the subject uppermost in all minds, which we give in full. He then delivered a short discourse on another subject. When he rose to pray he read the following : —

" Anthony Burns, now in prison and in danger of being sent into slavery, most earnestly asks your prayers, and that of your congregation, that God would remember him in his great distress and deliver him from this peril.

"From Rev. Mr. Grimes and Deacon Pitts, at Burns' special request."

He said, in substance, (we cannot give his language precisely,) that this was the old form for such requests, but he did not like it. It seemed to ask God to do our duty. God was never backward to do his work, and we should do ours. He could not ask God to work a miracle to deliver Anthony Burns, although if he should see fit to do so it should be accepted with proper sentiments of reverence and gratitude. He had received the same request in another form, which he liked better, and read as follows : —

" *To all the Christian Ministers of the Church of Christ in Boston.*

" Brothers : I venture humbly to ask an interest in your prayers and those of your congregations, that I may be restored to the natural and inalienable rights with which I am endowed by the Creator, and especially to the enjoyment of the blessings of liberty, which, it is said, this government was ordained to secure. ANTHONY BURNS.

" Boston Slave Pen, May 24, 1854."

The discourse which followed his " Lesson for the Day" was on the war now agitating Europe, and the rapacious and unprincipled spirit of the men who would hurry us into another war to aggrandize the slave power; but he had some allusions to the present state of things in Boston. Here is one of them : —

" Boston is in a state of siege to-day. We are living under military rule in order that we may serve the spirit of slavery; and Boston is hunting ground for the South who respects us so much. Our Nicholas is a Virginia kidnapper. Our ruler is a Judge of Probate."

A LESSON FOR THE DAY.

DELIVERED AT THE MUSIC HALL, SUNDAY, MAY 28, 1854.

BY REV. THEODORE PARKER.

[Phonographic report by Messrs. Slack and Yerrington.]

I see by the face of each one of you, as well as by the number of all, what is expected of me to-day. A young man, some time since, sent me a request, asking me, Cannot you extemporize a sermon for this day? It is easier to do than not to do it. But I shall not extemporize a *sermon* for to-day — I shall extemporize *the scripture*. I shall therefore pass by the Bible words, which I designed to read from the Old Testament and the New, and shall take the morning lesson from the circumstances of the past week. The time has not come for me to preach a sermon on the great wrong that is now enacting in this city. The deed is not done; any counsel I have to offer is better given elsewhere than here, at another time than now. Neither you nor I are quite calm enough to-day, to look the matter fairly in the face, and see entirely what it means. I had proposed to preach this morning, (before the events of the past week took place,) on the subject of WAR, taking my theme from the present commotions in Europe, which also will reach us, and have already. That will presently be the theme of my morning's sermon. Next Sunday I shall preach on the PERILS INTO WHICH AMERICA IS BROUGHT AT THIS DAY. That is the theme for *next* Sunday: the other is for *to-day*. But, before I proceed to that, I have some words to say in place of the Scripture lesson, after the fashion of the Old Testament prophets.

Since last we came together, there has been a MAN STOLEN in this city of our fathers. It is not the first, it may not be the last. He is now in the great slave pen of the city of Boston. He is there, if I understand it aright, against the law of the Commonwealth, which, if I am rightly informed, prohibits the use of State edifices as United States jails — I may be mistaken. Any forcible attempt to take him from that BARRACOON of Boston, would be wholly without use. For, besides the holiday soldiers that belong to the city of Boston, and are ready to shoot down their brothers in a just cause, or in an unjust cause, any day when the city government gives them its command and its liquor, I understand there are one hundred and eighty-four marines lodged in the court house, every man of them furnished with a musket and a bayonet, with his side arms and twenty-four ball cartridges. They are stationed, also, in a building very strong, and where five men, in a passage-way half the width of this pulpit, can defend it against five and twenty, or five hundred. To keep the peace, the Mayor, who, the other day, regretted the arrest of our brother, Anthony Burns, and declared that his sympathies were *wholly* with the alleged fugitive — and, of course, wholly *against* the claimant and the Marshal — in order to keep the peace of the city, the Mayor must become corporal of the guard for the kidnappers. He must keep the peace of our city, and defend these guests of Boston, over the graves, the unmonumented graves of John Hancock and Samuel Adams.

A man has been killed by violence. Some say he was killed by his own coadjutors. I could easily believe it. There is evidence enough that they were greatly frightened. These were not United States soldiers, but volunteers from the streets of Boston, who, for their pay, went into the court house to assist in kidnapping a brother man. They, I say, were so cowardly that they could not use the simple cutlasses they had in their hands, but smote right and left, like ignorant and frightened ruffians, as they were. They may have slain their brother, or not — I cannot tell. It is said by some that they killed him. Another story is, that he was killed by a hostile hand from without. Some said by a bullet, some by an axe, and others yet by a knife. As yet, nobody knows the facts. But a man has been killed. He was a volunteer in this service. He liked the business of enslaving a man, and has gone to render an account to God for his gratuitous work. Twelve men have been arrested, and are now in jail, to await their trial for *wilful* murder!

Here, then, is one man butchered, and twelve men brought in peril of their lives. Why is this? Whose fault is it? Some eight years ago, a Boston merchant, by his mercenaries, kidnapped a man between this city and Old Quincy, and carried him off. Boston mechanics, the next day, held up the half-eagles which they received as their pay for kidnapping a man. The matter was brought before the grand jury for the county of Suffolk, and abundant evidence was presented, as I understand, but they found "no bill." A wealthy merchant, in the name of trade, had stolen a black man, who, on board a ship, had come to this city, had been seized by the mercenaries of this merchant, kept by them for a while, and then, when he escaped, kidnapped a second time in the city of Boston. That was one thing. Boston did not punish the deed; the merchant lost no "personal popularity."

The Fugitive Slave bill was presented to us, and Boston rose up to welcome it. The greatest man in all the North came here, and in this city told Massachusetts she must obey the Fugitive Slave bill "with alacrity" — that we must all "conquer our prejudices" in favor of justice and the unalienable rights of man. Boston "conquered her prejudices" in favor of justice and the unalienable rights of man. Do you not remember the meeting that was held in Faneuil Hall, when a "political soldier of fortune," sometimes called "the Democratic Prince of the Devil," howled at the idea that there was a Law of God higher than the Fugitive Slave bill? He sneered, and asked, will you have the "Higher Law of God" to rule over you? and the multitude that occupied the floor, and the multitude that crowded the galleries, howled down the higher law of God! They treated the higher law to a laugh and a howl! That was Tuesday night. It was the Tuesday before Thanksgiving day. On that Thanksgiving day, I told the congregation that the men who howled down the higher law of Almighty God, had got Almighty God to settle with; that they had sown the wind, and would reap the whirlwind. At that meeting Mr. Choate told the people "REMEMBER! REMEMBER! *Remember!*" Then nobody knew what to "remember." Now you know. That is the state of that case.

Then you "REMEMBER" the kidnappers came here to seize Thomas Sims. Thomas Sims *was* seized. Nine days he was on trial for more than his life, and never saw a judge — never saw a jury. He was sent back into bondage from the city of Boston. You remember the chains that were put around the court house; you "REMEMBER" the judges of Massachusetts stooping, crouching, creeping, *crawling* under the chain of slavery, in order to get to their own courts. All these things you "REMEMBER." Boston was non-resistant. She gave her "back to the smiters" — from the South; she "withheld not her cheek" — from the scorn of South Carolina, and welcomed the "spitting" of kidnappers from Georgia and Virginia Now we are having our pay for it. To-day we have our pay for that conduct. You have not forgotten the "fifteen hundred gentlemen of property and standing," who volunteered to conduct Mr. Sims to slavery — Marshal Tukey's "gentlemen." They "remember" it. They are sorry enough now. Let us forgive — we need not forget. REMEMBER! REMEMBER! *Remember!*

The Nebraska bill has just now been passed. Who passed it? The fifteen hundred "gentlemen of property and standing" in Boston, who, in 1851, volunteered to carry Thomas Sims into slavery by force of arms. *They* passed the Nebraska bill. If Boston had punished the kidnapper of 1845, there would have been no Fugitive Slave bill in 1850. If Massachusetts in 1850 had declared the bill should not be executed, the kidnapper would never have shown his face in the streets of Boston. If, failing this, Boston had said, in 1851, "Thomas Sims shall not be carried off, and forsibly or peacefully, by the majesty of the great body of men, had resisted it, no kidnapper would have come here again. There would have been no Nebraska bill. But to every demand of the slave power, Massachusetts has said, "Yes! yes! — we grant it all!" "Agitation must cease!" "Save the Union!"

Southern slavery is an institution that is in earnest. Northern Freedom is an institution that is not in earnest. It was in earnest in '76 and '83. It has not been in earnest since. The Compromises are but provisional. Slavery is the only finality. Now, since the Nebraska bill is passed, an attempt is made to add insult to insult, injury to injury. There was a fugitive slave case at Syracuse this last week; at New York, a brother of Rev. Dr. Pennington, an established clergyman of large reputation, great character, acknowledged learning, who has his diploma from the University of Heidelburg, in Germany, — a more honorable source than that from which any clergyman in Massachusetts ever received his, — *his* brother and two nephews were kidnapped in New York, and without any trial, without any defence, were hurried off into bondage. Then at Boston, you know what was done in the last four days. Behold the consequences of the doctrine that there is no "higher law." Look at Boston, to-day. There are no chains around your court house — there are *ropes* around it. A hundred and eighty-four United States soldiers are there. They are, I am told, mostly foreigners — the scum of the earth, none but such enter into armies, as common soldiers, in a country like ours. I say it with pity — they are not to blame for having been born where they were and *what they are.* I pity the scum as well as I pity the mass of men. The accident of birth kept you and me from being among that same scum. The soldiers are there, I say, and their trade is to kill. Why is this so?

You remember the meeting at Faneuil Hall, last Friday, — when even the words of my friend Wendell Phillips, the most eloquent words that get spoken in America, in this century, hardly prevailed upon the multitude from going, and by violence attempting to storm the Court House. What stirred them up! It was the spirit of our fathers — the spirit of justice and liberty in your heart, and in my heart, and in the heart of all of us. Sometimes it gets the better of a man's prudence, especially on occasions like this, and so excited was that assembly of four or five thousand men, that even the words of eloquent Wendell Phillips could hardly restrain them from going at once rashly to the Court House and tearing it to the ground.

Boston is the most peaceful of cities. Why? Because we have commonly had a place that was worth keeping. No city respects laws so much. Because the laws have been made by the people, for the people, and are laws which respect justice. Here is a law which the people would not keep. It is a law of our Southern masters, a law not fit to keep.

Why is Boston in this confusion to-day? The fugitive slave bill Commissioner has just now been sowing the wind, that we may reap the whirlwind. The old fugitive slave bill Commissioner stands back; he has gone to look after his "personal popularity." But when Commissioner Curtis does not dare appear in this matter, another man comes forward, and for the first time seeks to kidnap his man in the city of Boston. Judge Loring is a man whom I respected and honored. His private life is wholly blameless, so far as I know. He has been, I think, uniformly beloved. His character has entitled him to the esteem of his fellow citizens. I have known him somewhat. I never heard a mean word from him — many good words. He was once the law partner of Horace

Mann, and learned humanity of a great teacher — have respected him a good deal. He is a *respectable* man — in the Boston sense of that word, and in a much higher sense: at least, I thought so. He is a kind-hearted, charitable man: a good neighbor; a fast friend — when politics do not interfere; charitable with his purse; an excellent husband; a kind father; a good relative. And I should as soon have expected that venerable man who sits before me, born before your Revolution [SAMUEL MAY] — I should as soon have expected *him* to go and kidnap Robert Morris, or any other of the colored men I see around me, as I should have expected Judge Loring to do this thing. But he has sown the wind, and we are reaping the whirlwind. I need not say what I now think of him. He is to act to-morrow, and may yet act like a man. Let us wait and see. Perhaps there is manhood in him yet. But, my friends, all this confusion is *his* work. He knew he was *stealing a man*, born with the same right to life, liberty and the pursuit of happiness as himself. He knew the slaveholders had no more right to Anthony Burns than to his own daughter. He knew the consequences of stealing a man in Boston. He knew that there are men in Boston who have not yet conquered their prejudices — men who respect the higher law of God. He knew there would be a meeting at Faneuil Hall — gatherings in the street. He knew there would be violence.

EDWARD GREELEY LORING, Judge of Probate for the county of Suffolk, in the State of Massachusetts, Fugitive Slave Bill Commissioner of the United States, before these citizens of Boston, on Ascension Sunday, assembled to worship God, I charge you with the death of that man who was murdered on last Friday night. He was your fellow servant in kidnapping. He dies at your hand. You fired the shot which makes his wife a widow, his child an orphan. I charge you with the peril of twelve men, arrested for murder and on trial for their lives; I charge you with filling the Court House with one hundred and eighty-four hired ruffians of the United States, and alarming not only this city for her liberties that are in peril, but stirring up the whole Commonwealth of Massachusetts with indignation, which no man knows how to stop — which no man can stop. You have done it all!

This is my lesson for the day.

THE FUGITIVE SLAVE EXCITEMENT.

We have endeavored to lay before our readers a true and faithful account of the events which have occurred here within the last three days connected with the arrest and examination of an alleged fugitive from slavery named Anthony Burns. The popular excitement still continues; and at the present moment, as the examination is progressing, a dense crowd is gathered about the Court House, actuated chiefly, as we presume, by motives of curiosity; but in respect to many, no doubt, by a desire and a determination, if circumstances should favor it, to resist even by violence the operation of the law. It is observed that many, perhaps the larger portion, of this crowd are strangers. While our own citizens, as a general thing, are properly engaged in their customary avocations, means have been taken elsewhere, and particularly in Worcester, to induce people to lay aside their business and come to the city to add fuel to the flame of excitement here. Meanwhile the United States and the city authorities have taken such steps as it is to be hoped will check any further violence. The United States armed forces, which have been called in, are to aid directly in the execution of the law. The precautionary measures taken by the city authorities are to preserve the peace of the city, by whomsoever it may be disturbed. In addition to the ordinary police force, a military force, under the direction of

Major General Edmands, will be available for prompt and efficient service, if unfortunately such service should be needed. Cheated as we have been by the South, and grating as is the duty of acquiescence in this odious law, we earnestly hope that no violence will attend its execution.

It is not by lawless violence and bloodshed that we can manifest the deep indignation which pervades the public mind at the recent act of treachery on the part of the South in repudiating their part of a solemn compromise, and in leaving us to fulfil, at the hazard of our own honor, the hateful agreement to which we had bound ourselves in the vain hope of a final adjustment of the threatening controversies between the free and slaveholding states. Let us rather set an example, not only of faithfulness and honor, but of submission to an offensive compact, and reserve all the energies of an insulted and disgusted public sentiment for a lawful and constitutional demonstration, such as shall convince the South that there is a point of forbearance beyond which we cannot go.

All remained quiet during last night in the vicinity of the Court House, and but few arrests were made.

Court Square has been crowded during the forenoon; and a large number of strangers from the surrounding towns and cities are arriving by every train. Among them was a procession of about three hundred from Worcester, carrying a banner with the inscription, "Worcester Freedom Club."

The Boston City Grays, Captain French, are quartered at the City Hall; they will be relieved to-night by another of our city military companies. The United States marines from the Navy Yard, and one company of United States artillery from Fort Independence, are also quartered in the Court House.

The excitement outside continued this morning, although the crowd was not large until eleven o'clock.

Among the rumors of the morning was one that several car loads of persons had come down from points on the Worcester Railroad to take part in the proceedings. There was also another, that one thousand five hundred members of a prominent club in this city had volunteered their services to aid in the preservation of order and the execution of the laws; also, that threats of personal violence to several of the officers had been made by certain persons, going so far as an intimation that one of the officers who arrested the fugitive would be shot before night.

Workmen have been employed during the forenoon in repairing the damage to the Court House of Friday night.

Mr. John C. Cluer, who was arrested on Saturday last for a breach of the peace, was brought up for examination and committed.

Handbills have been widely circulated and posted up in the various towns in the vicinity of Boston, and in Lynn, Salem, Worcester, and other distant places, inviting "the yoemanry of New England" to come in by the early trains to Boston on Monday and rally in Court Square, to "lend the moral weight of your presence and the aid of your counsel to the friends of justice and humanity in the city." Many unthinking persons have responded to this appeal and are in Court Square, helping to swell the mob which has there gathered. We do not know that any further unlawful attempt is to be made to rescue the fugitive Burns. We hope that the bloodshed of Friday night, and the opportunity which has since been afforded for deliberate reflection, has calmed the heated passions of those who have incited to riot, and that wiser counsels now prevail. But if our hopes should prove unfounded, if the sanguinary counsels of the speakers in Faneuil Hall are to be acted upon by their deluded followers, we would most earnestly appeal to every good citizen — every friend of order and every one who respects the laws — to keep away from Court Square. Remember that those who are drawn together by curiosity do indeed "lend the moral weight of their presence" to deeds of lawless violence. Remember that any attempt to rescue Burns by forcible means is hopeless. He is surrounded by a wall of bristling bayonets and of guns loaded with powder and ball. Not only the United States troops, but the citizen soldiery will do their duty. An attack upon the officers of the law, supported by such a force, would be not only profitless but fool-hardy, and the consequences would inevitably be deplorable.

We say, most earnestly, to those who are attracted by mere curiosity and who do not sympathize with the law breakers, that, if bloodshed occurs, you may be the first victims; and, if you escape, to the extent that your presence gives encouragement to the evil-disposed, *you will be accessory to the death of those who fall.* We repeat, *let every good citizen go quietly about his business, and leave the avenues leading to the Court House to the evil-disposed and riotous.*

"Edward Greeley Loring, Judge of Probate for the county of Suffolk, in the State of Massachusetts, Fugitive Slave Bill Commissioner of the United States, before these citizens of Boston, on Ascension Sunday, assembled to worship God, I charge you with the death of that man who was murdered on last Friday night. He was your fellow servant in kidnapping. He dies at your hand. You fired the shot which makes his wife a widow, his child an orphan."

The above we extract from a report of the inflammatory *sermon* (!) delivered by the Rev. Theodore Parker yesterday before his congregation in the new Music Hall. Let us see where rests the responsibility, before God and man, for this murder. In one position we probably agree with Mr. Parker. It was not the person who, in a moment of intense excitement, inflicted the fatal stab upon the person of James Batchelder, who is responsible for this deed; *but it is the men who artfully inflamed his passions, and then left him to their uncontrolled exercise.* It is they alone who are GUILTY OF MURDER, and they alone who, here or hereafter, must answer for the unhallowed deed. The law may not be able to reach them, but public opinion will; and their own consciences, when they find time to listen to them, will say to each and every one of them, when the question is asked, Who is guilty of murder? — "*Thou art the man.*"

There was not a man on the rostrum of Faneuil Hall on Friday evening whose hands are not dyed in the blood of James Batchelder; but if any one is more guilty than another, it is the Rev. Theodore Parker, for it was he who put the motion to adjourn to Court Square. They may all thank heaven that his is the only life they have to answer for. We trust that this sad tragedy may be a serious warning to these agitators, and that those who are in the habit of listening to, and being excited by, their inflammatory railings, will at least follow the example which they set them on Friday night, of *retiring quietly to bed* after their speeches were over, instead of joining the mob which they had incited to deeds of violence.

FURTHER ARRESTS AND INCIDENTS.

THE PRESIDENT'S INSTRUCTIONS TO THE UNITED STATES MARSHAL.

We are happy to announce that there has been no repetition of the scenes of violence enacted on Friday evening at the Court House. The firmness of the authorities, together with the presence of a large body of military, has sufficed to keep the riotously disposed in order, and, although hosts of people have been at all times in the vicinity of Court Square, there has been no outbreak. Our reporters furnish us with the following record of facts and incidents connected with the affair since our issue of Saturday evening.

Throughout Saturday afternoon great excitement prevailed in Court Square, the crowd numbering several thousands, although at about four o'clock the number was evidently less than at any other period.

John C. Cluer was arrested in Court Street, near the Court House, about three o'clock Saturday afternoon, by Constable Spoor, on a warrant from the Police Court, charging him, with ten others, with the murder of James Batchelder, and was committed to jail to await examination, which will probably take place to-morrow. John Morrison was also arrested and committed on the same charge. These we believe make eleven of the rioters who are charged with murder.

Saturday forenoon a middle-aged woman named Hinckley, well dressed in black and of very reputable demeanor, posted herself near the easterly entrance of the Court House and demanded admission, but the officers on duty politely refused compliance with her demand. She continued to maintain her positon for two or three hours, demanding admission, but all to no purpose. The officers declared this to be the most persevering and remarkable case of feminine curiosity which had ever fallen under their observation. Having exhausted her vocabulary of argument, and finding that there was "no use in knocking at the door," she quietly left the square.

As Mr. William C. Fay was conversing in the Square with a friend, about half past five o'clock Saturday P. M., a stalwart colored man named Nelson Hopewell, (who by his previous actions had attracted the attention of the officers) interfered, and aimed a blow at Mr. Fay. Officer Tarleton instantly seized Hopewell, and a violent tussle ensued for a moment, when both fell to the ground. Officers J. H. Riley, Cheswell, and Rogers, came to the rescue, and Hopewell was hurried to the watch house, Mr. Tarleton retaining his hold of him throughout. Hopewell had a belt around his body, and attached to the belt was a leather sheath which held an African knife, called a *creese*, the blade to which is some ten inches long, curved and slender, and bore upon it distinct stains of blood.

It appears from the *post mortem* examination of the body of the unfortunate Batchelder, that he was *not* killed by a pistol shot, but that the mortal wound was inflicted by a long and sharp instrument, near the groin, penetrating the body six or seven inches, and severing the main arteries. The *creese* is capable of inflicting just such a wound as Mr. Batchelder received, but there is no testimony yet made known which connects Hopewell with the outrage of Friday night.

The wife of Mr. Batchelder knew nothing of his death until Saturday morning, when the announcement was made to her by a lady who saw the account of the occurrence in the morning papers. She chanced to be in the front yard, and immediately fainted and was taken into the house.

A man named Alfred Swain, belonging in Lynn, made himself conspicuous during Saturday afternoon, by haranguing the crowd, but he was speedily cut short in his remarks by the Police, who furnished him with less crowded quarters in the watch house. After a short confinement, and under his assurance that he would take the first train for Lynn, he was released from custody.

Major General Edmands and staff established their quarters at the Albion on Saturday morning, previous to which he had received the precept for calling out the Boston companies, and the Independent Corps of Cadets, Lieutenant Colonel T. C. Amory commanding, and the Boston Light Infantry, Captain Rogers, were called out to preserve order and prevent any breach of the public peace. The Cadets remained on duty through Saturday night, but previous to leaving the Square and repairing to their quarters at the Albion, the Mayor, upon being introduced to the corps, briefly addressed them, expressing his confidence in their efficiency and honesty of purpose, and remarking upon the orderly spirit generally manifested by the citizens.

The Light Infantry remained on duty in the Square until a few minutes past 9 o'clock Saturday evening, when they were relieved by the New England Guards, Captain Henshaw, who quartered in City Hall, where they remained until yesterday A. M., when they were relieved by the Union Guards, Captain Brown. A Corporal's Guard continues stationed at each of the armories.

About half past seven o'clock Saturday evening, Chief of Police Taylor and Deputy Chief Ham, with a strong force of officers, commenced clearing the Square, and very shortly, and without disturbance, the work was accomplished. Ropes were stretched across each avenue leading to the Square, and officers were stationed to prevent all persons excepting such as had special business within the square, from passing inside of the lines. Many who had composed the crowd gradually withdrew, and at half past ten o'clock, P. M., but a few hundred persons remained in the vicinity; and many of these were colored people of both sexes, but at a later hour they also retired peaceably to their homes.

Mayor Smith remained at the City Hall during the fore part of Saturday night, superintending the measures adopted to preserve the peace.

The Chief of Police and his Deputy, together with their under officers, have, through the whole affair, thus far, been unceasing in their arduous duties, and have proved themselves men of nerve and officers of determination in the faithful and prompt discharge of their duties. The whole Police Department were on duty through the night, ready for any emergency. Saturday evening, Lewis Osgood, Thomas Farretty, James Bellows, (upon whom was found a dirk knife), Joseph Brown, James Cunningham, and Charles H. Crickney were arrested for riotous conduct in front of the Court House, and were committed to jail. Since nine o'clock on Friday and up to 12 o'clock on Saturday night, fifty persons were arrested and placed in the centre watch-house, and with few exceptions, the arrests were made for riotous and disorderly conduct about the Court House. Seventeen of those arrested were committed to Jail — the others being discharged after a short imprisonment.

Owing to a report which gained currency on Saturday afternoon, to the effect that an attack was to be made that evening on the residences of Theodore Parker, 1 Essex place, and Wendell Phillips, 26 Essex street, quite a number of persons, probably from motives of curiosity, slowly passed and re-passed Essex street during the evening until a late hour, but no attempt was made at a breach of the peace. This is but one of the many groundless rumors which have prevailed since Saturday noon.

Between twelve and one o'clock on Saturday night, as a carriage containing Hon. B. F. Hallett and his son Henry L. Hallett, was passing up School street, two colored men were observed following and closely watching it. They soon hailed the driver, and the carriage was stopped. Deputy Chief Ham and officer Pritchard were close at hand, and upon being observed by the negroes, the latter took to their heels. The Messrs. Hallett alighted from the carriage, and were accompanied home by Deputy Ham, while officer Pritchard gave chase to the negroes, and succeeded in arresting one of them, but he was subsequently discharged from custody. The man gave his name as James Palm.

U. S. Marshal Freeman has received a telegraphic despatch from the President of the United States, to the effect that he (the Marshal) had performed his duty, and instructing him to continue so to do.

Our city, yesterday, was in a state of excitement almost unparalleled. The abolitionists and their confederates did all they could, to subserve the cause of mob law! Their treasonable meeting at Faneuil Hall was not enough. It was not enough that Parker, and Phillips, and their associates, excited the passions of their deluded dupes up to the pitch of destruction and murder, nor that seditious handbills stared the passers by at the corners of the streets. Bodies of men, from distant towns, came in to the city, to aid their detestable work, and the consequence was, that all day our city was the scene of great confusion.

What these bold, bad men are doing, is nothing more nor less than committing treason. The following extract from Daniel Webster's speech at Albany, 1851, delineates their crime. He said:—

"The act of taking away Shadrach from the public authorities in Boston, and sending him off, was an act of clear treason. I speak this in the hearing of men who are lawyers; I speak it out to the country; I say it every where, on my professional reputation. It was treason, and nothing less; that is to say, if men get together, and combine together, and resolve that they will oppose a law of the government, not in any one case, but in all cases; I say if they resolve to resist the law, whoever may be attempted to be made the subject of it, and carry that purpose into effect, by resisting the application of the law in any one case, either by force of arms or force of numbers, that, sir, is treason. (Turning to Mr. Spencer, and stamping with emphasis.) You know it well. (Continuing to address Mr. Spencer.) The resolution itself, unacted on, is not treason; it only manifests a treasonable purpose. When this purpose is proclaimed — and it is proclaimed that it will be carried out in all cases — and is carried into effect, by force of arms or numbers, in any one case, that constitutes a case of levying war against the Union."

The present case is a parallel case. Burns is in the hands of the law. Those who engage in the work of attempting to take him away from the officers, will commit treason against their country, and must suffer its penalties. Is there a doubt as to this? We appeal to citizens to lay aside their prejudices; to forget partizan opinions; to look at this treasonable movement of Parker, Phillips, and their abettors, in its true light. They aim to give this city over to mob rule; they intend treason against their country! What can be worse? Citizens of Boston! let patriotism, loyalty to law, the recollections of the past, regard for the present, the good name and fame of this place, have their course! Resolve to trample, as with a strong hand, on this treason, and to support an administration of the law!

The attempt in the board of aldermen, yesterday, to eject the United States authorities from the court house, failed by the casting vote of the mayor. This disgraceful design to administer to the spirit of tumult and disorder, will receive the indignant rebuke of all patriotic men. It evinces the mad excess to which fanatical passion will carry those who surrender themselves to its control, and the danger of trusting public authority to individuals devoid of a proper sense of their obligations as guardians of the welfare and safety of the city.

THE AID OF THE UNITED STATES TROOPS TO THE MARSHAL.

The facts in regard to the requisition of the marshal, for the United States troops to aid in executing the laws, were stated by Mr. Hallett, the United States attorney, in the hearing, yesterday, before the commissioner, of the matter of the fugitive Burns.

Mr. Ellis, of counsel for the party under examination, made a verbal protest to the commissioner against proceeding, on the pretext that the marshal had unlawfully employed United States troops to guard the passageways to the court house, and had packed the court room with friends of the law, and he wished them removed and the court held elsewhere.

The United States attorney (B. F. Hallett,) rose, and said that the protest made by the counsel, (Mr. Ellis,) not being a matter in the course of the examination, but implicating the conduct of the marshal and the United States officers, for the measures taken to preserve order in and around this court, he felt bound to reply as the law officer of the United States, and as counsel for the United States marshal.

The commissioner said it was unnecessary, as he had decided that the examination was to proceed, and there was no motion before the court.

Mr. Hallett said he was aware of that, but the United States marshal had been openly charged here, by the counsel, (Mr. Ellis,) with unlawfully packing this court room and stopping the passageways with armed men, and such language, if uttered here, should be replied to. He desired to say that the United States soldiers were here in aid of the marshal, to enable him to preserve order in this court, and to execute the laws, and that they were summoned here as a part of the *posse comitatus*, under a certificate of the judge of the United States district court, (Judge Sprague.)

The men who committed murder that night came directly from the incitements to riot and bloodshed, which had maddened them in that hall; and it was then, and before he knew of the murder, that he, as United States attorney, called on Judge Sprague late at night, and upon his representation and his own judgment of the necessity, Judge Sprague issued the certificate upon which the marshal called in the United States troops and others to his aid, and they promptly met the requisition.

The President of the United States has approved of this course, and the efficient aid which the marshal has, both armed and unarmed, to prevent further violence and murder, are here by the sanction of the President, and under a certificate of a judge of the United States courts, and therefore it is a proceeding not only necessary, but such as the commissioner himself, and all good citizens, are bound to respect.

The Boston Journal comes out manfully in maintenance of the laws, and sustains the cause of public order, at this crisis when resistance is threatened and anarchy and confusion are boldly preached to the people. Capt. Charles O. Rogers, commander of the Boston Light Infantry, one of the companies that have been on duty, is one of the publishers of the Journal, from which we copy the following pointed expression of opinion as to the guilt incurred in the killing of Mr. Batchelder:—

" Let us see where rests the responsibility, before God and man, for this murder. In one position we probably agree with Mr. Parker. It was not the person who, in a moment of intense excitement, inflicted the fatal stab upon the person of James Batchelder, who is responsible for this deed; *but it is the men who artfully inflamed his passions, and then left him to their uncontrolled exercise.* It is they alone who are GUILTY of MURDER, and they alone who—here or hereafter—must answer for the unhallowed deed. The law may not be able to reach them, but public opinion will, and their own consciences—when they find time to listen to them—will say to each and every one of them, when the question is asked, Who is guilty of murder?—' *Thou art the man.*' "

There was not a man on the rostrum at Faneuil Hall, on Friday evening, whose hands are not dyed in the blood of James Batchelder; but, if any one is more guilty than another, it is the Rev. Theodore Parker, for it was he who first put the motion to adjourn to Court square. They may all thank heaven that his is the only life they have to answer for. We trust that this sad tragedy may be a serious warning to these agitators, and that those who are in the habit of listening to and of being excited by their inflammatory railings, will at least follow the example which they set them on Friday night, of *retiring quietly to bed*, after their speeches were over, instead of joining the mob they had incited to deeds of violence.

The ropes were removed yesterday, and the people having free access to Court square, thronged it during the day.

It was stated in Court square that Mr. Suttle, the claimant of Burns, had peremptorily refused to sell him on any terms, and that the negotiations had all been stopped. A violent handbill, of the tenor of that issued the day before, was posted about the streets denying the sale.

Every thing seemed to wear a quiet aspect, but there was a deep feeling beneath, and groups that talked calmly, looked restless and chafed, as if they were anxious for a rupture.

The Bay State Club tendered the United States Marshal 1500 men to enforce the laws.

The City Guards, Captain French, were on duty yesterday, at City Hall, having relieved the Union Guards.

A difficulty has been experienced in finding food for the soldiers. The eating houses in the square were thronged with visitors, and Mr. J. B. Smith's colored waiters refused to prepare food for the military.

At about twelve o'clock, a party from Worcester, numbering about two' hundred, arrived in the city, and marched through the streets, with a banner flying, denoting that the "Worcester Freedom Club" was among us to set matters to rights. They were not a very handsome set of men, and bore nothing very intimidating in their looks. After marching about the court house they repaired to the Tremont Temple, and spent the time until half past one o'clock in listening to addresses and proposing plans of action, when they adjourned to meet in Court square at three o'clock, there to march around the court house every half hour, to "keep the peace, and do a little something for freedom at the same time." The party was headed by Dr. Martin, of Worcester. Among those present, were William L. Garrison, Stephen Foster, Charles Lenox Remond, and other prominent abolitionists. Addresses were made by some of these. S. P. Hanscom stated that one of the coroners had a writ of some kind to take Burns, which he would serve if he could obtain sufficient force; and Hanscom called for volunteers to aid the coroner, but the volunteers didn't come. Hanscom also stated that there was a secret committee in session somewhere, but declined to answer questions on the subject.

It was easy to get up cheers among the crowd, and Governor Washburn, chief executive magistrate, became the recipient of six cheers from the abolitionists, upon the assurance that he was with them in spirit.

Mr. Stephen S. Foster addressed the meeting, in which he avowed himself a non-resistant, and argued for a moral rather than a physical demonstration, but was ready to bare his breast, if need be, to the bayonet or the ball. If his life or those of a few others were sacrificed, to accomplish the end proposed, it would be a glorious bargain even at such a price. Mr. Garrison was rather more lukewarm. He had been engaged in the same business so long that his zeal for martyrdom had become rather blunted, and he didn't feel like rushing towards it.

[We will state, in connection with this Worcester valor, that when it was found necessary to take their banner from them because of the confusion its appearing caused about the square, two policemen removed it very easily without the least resistance. The banner was placed in the police station.]

The following is a copy of one of the infamous incendiary handbills that were posted about town :—

"*Murderers, Thieves and Blacklegs Employed by Marshal Freeman !!* — Marshal Freeman has been able to stoop low, enough to insult even the United States marines, by employing murderers, prize-fighters, thieves, three card monte men and gambling-house keepers to aid him in the rendition of Burns.

[Here follow the names of some of the Marshal's assistants.]

These are the characters with whom the officers of the United States marines are called upon to act. Let the people mark them! They are in the court house. They are petted by hunker democrats. They are supplied with money and rum by the United States, by order of Marshal Freeman! Such scoundrels, freemen of Massachusetts, are employed to trample upon our laws and insult you, and are supplied with arms and ammunition to shoot you down, if you dare to assert your just rights. Will you submit quietly to such insults!"

Reverend Mr. Fogg, a Baptist clergyman and abolitionist, from New Hampshire, finding but a very meagre assembly in Tremont Temple, deliberately expressed the opinion that his friends were a set of cowards.

It was stated yesterday, that a United States government vessel was to be fitted out, to take Burns back to Virginia, in the event of his being given up by the Court.

Thomas Sweeney, in the Herald, repudiating John C. Cluer as an Irishman, as stated in one of the papers, says, —

" Since the passage of that questionable enactment, the fugitive slave law, it has been openly and violently resisted, and violated in this city and elsewhere, by the descendants of the Puritans only — but in no instance have Irish adopted citizens coöperated with them. The citizens of Boston, of Irish birth, have taken a solemn oath to sustain the Constitution and laws of this glorious Union — and, to their honor be it spoken, they never have, and never will be found to act inconsistently with the proper observance of that solemn obligation."

It will be seen that an order was introduced in the board of Mayor and Aldermen for clearing the court house of the troops quartered there, which was defeated by the Mayor's vote.

At half-past seven o'clock the chief of police gave the order for clearing Court square, and in ten minutes the entire square was as clear of a crowd as ever it was upon a Sunday. The contrast was very marked between the order that prevailed and the crowded and active appearance that had been presented a few minutes previous. It required but about seventy policemen to effect this change, and it either proved that the mob was not violently disposed, or that the force of the law was very mighty when backed by stalwart and resolute men.

The least opposition was a signal for arrest, and one young man — James H. Fowler, of Cambridgeport — who attempted a speech savoring rather strongly of the heated, in front of the court house, was passed speedily to the station house, all the way clamoring about violated rights.

Rumors were rife of arrivals from New Bedford and other places, with reinforcements for the mob, and the cars brought many people, though whether they came with the intention supposed, is not known.

The anniversary meetings call many persons to the city, and suspicion, excited to the utmost degree, makes small distinction.

Last evening two or three men crowded over the line at the entrance of Court square, from Court street, and were put out by the officers. During the scuffle that ensued, something fell upon the pavement with a ringing sound, which was afterwards found to be a piece of quarter inch wire, about a foot long, with one end bent in a ring, and ground at the other end, on four sides, to a point perfectly sharp. It was an ugly looking weapon. The one who dropped it escaped.

The evening passed off quietly. Large numbers remained in Court square till a late hour, but no disturbance occurred.

At 1 o'clock all still.

Yesterday there were more people in town than on Saturday, every train that arrived being crowded. Most of the strangers went up to the Court House, took a good look at its solid walls, its massive doors, and its ponderous pillars ; stared at the police who guarded every approach, speculated on the probable success ten thousand men would have in an attempt to rescue a prisoner, spent a few shillings for a dinner, and went home, perfectly satisfied, as a general thing, that there is physical force enough in Boston to execute the laws. — We give below a full account of the various incidents attending this exciting case since our paper of yesterday morning.

MOVEMENTS AND INCIDENTS YESTERDAY.

MONDAY, May 29.

This morning the Union Guards, Capt. Brown, who went on duty yesterday morning, and quartered in City Hall through the day and last night, were this morning relieved by the City Guard, Capt. French.

All was quiet in the vicinity of the Court House throughout last night, and has remained comparatively so this forenoon, no arrests for disorderly conduct or other offences having been made.

The woman, Hinckley, who we have already noticed, reappeared this morning and urged in vain her right to admission inside of the Court House. She left apparently disgusted with the officers.

At about noon considerable cheering was heard in Court Square. It proved to have been occasioned by the arrival of a band of men, numbering perhaps 200, bearing a banner on which was inscribed " Worcester Freedom Club." They marched up Court Street, into Court Square, and around the Court House, and from thence toward the west part of the city. It was a mixed club, many of the number being colored individuals, and some of them must have found themselves in strange company. A few moments after they left the Square, all was as quiet as previous to their appearance.

About one o'clock this afternoon a " gentleman from the country," as he termed himself, was arrested in front of the Court House and taken to Police Station No 1. Williams Court. He had imbibed so reely of intoxicating drink, as to be unable to take care of himself, so the Police kindly placed him where he could become sober.

We understand that the Bay State Club have tendered the U. S. Marshal 1500 men, to enforce the law.

MEETING IN THE MEIONAON.

A meeting composed principally of individuals from the country, is now (half-past one o'clock P. M.) in session in Meionaon Hall, over which Dr. Mitchell, of Worcester is presiding,

Wm. Lloyd Garrison and others of similar stamp have made inflammatory addresses. A Mr. Hanscom, who created such an excitement in New Bedford a year or two ago, stated that a writ of replevin, or habeas corpus, to take the fugitive Burns out of the custody of the United States Marshal, had been placed in the hands of one of the Coroners of Suffolk, who would serve it, provided he could obtain sufficient force to aid him.

The speaker was evidently much excited, and called for volunteers to aid the said Coroner. A large number of the persons present signified their willingness by rising from their seats, but subsequently, when Mr. Hanscom called upon them to " walk up to the rostrum and enroll their names," very few obeyed the call.

Mr. Hanscom also intimated that a select and secret Committee was in secret session in an ante-room, but declined giving the names of the Committee, when publicly requested so to do.

Cheers were given for various individuals, among whom was his Excellency Governor Washburn, for whom six cheers were given, upon the assurance from the Chairman that that functionary was with them in spirit and sentiment.

THE LIGHT DRAGOONS ORDERED OUT.

The Independent corps of Cadets, Lieutenant Colonel Amory, and the Boston Light Dragoons, Captain Wright, are now, (half past two o'clock P. M.,) assembling at their respective armories, having been ordered out by Major General Edmands.

BOYS IN BAD BUSINESS.

About 3 o'clock P. M., a band of boys, some 20 in number, wearing paper caps and headed by a miniature drum, marched through Court square and around the Court House.

It was understood that they were "determined to rescue the fugitive," and their appearance (whether formidable or otherwise) had the effect of drawing a large portion of the crowd after them.

The crowd in and about Court Square at about three o'clock was estimated at not less than seven or eight thousand persons.

BANNER OF THE WORCESTER FREEDOM CLUB SEIZED BY THE POLICE.

About quarter past three o'clock this afternoon a delegation of "gentlemen from the country," bearing a beautiful silk banner and two large yellow paper placards entered the westerly avenue from Court street, passed through the square and around the Court House, and repeated the same route, but as they reached the southerly end of the square Deputy Chief Ham with two or three officers took possession of the banner and placards, and deposited them in Police Station No. 1.

The silk banner bore the following inscriptions:

"Worcester Freedom Club — Warm Hearts and Fearless Souls — True to the Union and Constitution."

On the reverse:

"Freedom, National Liberty, Equality and Fraternity."

[Figure of the Goddess of Liberty.]

"Slavery Sectional."

Each of the two placards bore the following:

"Shall Freedom or Slavery Triumph?"

"Let Massachusetts speak."

The crowd at this time (half past five o'clock, P. M.) is as large as it has been at any time since the arrest of the fugitive, but so far to-day, there has been no serious outbreak.

Long before the hour assigned for the hearing of the case of Anthony Burns, the Court room was filled with an interesting and attentive company, composed principally of the same parties as on Saturday. At 10 o'clock, Commissioner Loring took his seat. After a little delay for the appearance of counsel, the proceedings were commenced.

C. M. Ellis, Esq., for the defence, protested against the proceeding, not on personal grounds, but because it was not right and fit. The prisoner had nothing to complain of in regard to his Honor's indulgence. He asked if it was fit while counsel bore arms. He said it was a shame that he should be forced to appear as counsel under such circumstances. It was not fit that the prisoner should sit with shackles on his arms. [An officer — He has not them on.] That is all right then, now, so far as that is concerned, but he was shackled on the first day. We protest, also, that we are not to come here to be reminded by force of the claims of the Constitution and the laws.

This room has been *packed* with armed men, and it is not fit that an examination should proceed. We protest, also, against conducting this case, when all its avenues and apartments are filled with military, making it difficult for any friends of the prisoner to obtain access. It was but fit that every one here present should bear the semblance of humanity upon his countenance, and the conduct of a man in his person. But though not denying that some friends enter as an act of courtesy where they have a right, the object seems to be, for some cause, that the countenances about, instead of reflecting the benignity that ought to be shed from a tribunal of justice, shall only stare on it with hate. The Commissioner had said on Saturday he knew nothing relative to the prisoner, as then prejudicial to his freedom; and he hoped that all the proceedings would be conducted on that supposition till otherwise properly, calmly and legally shown.

COMMISSIONER LORING.—The examination should proceed. I will give this consideration if necessary, hereafter.

B. F. Hallett, Esq., United States Attorney, rose and commented on the remarks of Mr. Ellis. He said that the protest made by the counsel (Mr. Ellis) not being a matter in the course of the examination, but implicating the conduct of the marshal and the United States officers for the measures taken to preserve order in and around this court, he felt bound to reply as the law officer of the United States and as counsel for the United States marshal, at whose request he was present.

The commissioner said it was unnecessary, as he had decided that the examination was to proceed, and there was no motion before the court.

Mr. Hallett said he was aware of that; but the United States marshal had been openly charged here by the counsel (Mr. Ellis) with unlawfully packing this court room and stopping the passage ways with armed men, and such language, if uttered here, should be replied to. He desired to say that the United States soldiers were here in aid of the marshal, to enable him to preserve order in this court and to execute the laws, and that they were summoned here as a part of the *posse comitatus*, under a certificate of the judge of the United States district court, (Judge Sprague.)

That proceeding was rendered necessary by the conduct of men who got up and inflamed the meeting at Faneuil Hall, some of whom he saw here within the bar, and who were claimed by the counsel (Mr. Ellis) as his friends. The men who committed murder that night came directly from the incitements to riot and bloodshed which had maddened them in that hall; and it was then, and before he knew of the murder, that he, as United States attorney, called on Judge Sprague late at night, and upon this representation, and his own judgment of the necessity, Judge Sprague issued the certificate upon which the marshal called in the United States troops to his aid, and they promptly met the requisition.

The President of the United States has approved of this course, and the efficient aid which the marshal has, both armed and unarmed, to prevent further violence and murder, are here by the sanction of the President, and under a certificate of a judge of the United States courts; and therefore it is a proceeding, not only necessary, but such as the commissioner himself and all good citizens are bound to respect.

Mr. Ellis, in response, was about to comment on Mr. Hallett's language, when the commissioner said that was a matter in which he alone was interested.

Mr. Ellis then asked for a delay till the circumstances of which he had spoken and complained were removed.

The commissioner replied that the trial must proceed.

Mr. Ellis then asked, in the absence of any record, whether the commissioner had any jurisdiction in this case. Mr. Loring replied that he was qualified fifteen years ago by Judge Story.

Mr. Parker, for the claimant, asked if it was necessary to go over the evidence already presented.

The commissioner replied that he did not deem it necessary.

Mr. Dana, for the defence, replied that the previous examination was when the prisoner had no counsel, and he inferred that the examination should now commence as though the arrest had just been made, he having no notes of the previous testimony given.

In reply, the court decided the complaint should be read, and the proceedings commenced anew.

The complaint was then read by Mr. Parker.

William Brent was then called as a witness, and testified that he was a merchant of Richmond, Va; was acquainted with Colonel Charles F. Suttle, and had been for a long time; knew Anthony Burns; the black man in court was the same — the prisoner at the bar; he knew Burns in Stafford county, and bore the relation of a slave to a master, being hired out by Suttle; had hired him himself in 1846, '47, and '48, or '47, '48, and '49, and knew of his being hired out since that time; hired him out last year and the present year, as agent for Colonel Suttle, in Richmond; the wages went to Colonel Suttle; knew him as a slave for twelve or fifteen years; last year, in March, was hired in Richmond by a Mr. Millspaugh, Mr. Suttle receiving the wages; the first letting of Burns by Suttle, to his knowledge, was the year previous to his hiring him himself; when not let out he lived with Colonel Suttle; previous to his being hired, he was a big boy, not capable of doing anything; there was no other Anthony Burns about the places resorted to by Suttle; he had a scar upon his right cheek and a cut across his right hand; there were no other marks upon him that he knew; he is about six feet high; I was born within three miles of Colonel Suttle; knew him ever since he could recollect; knew all his family; last saw Burns the Sunday previous to his absence — the 20th of March; he was missing on the 24th; I left Virginia on Saturday week morning; does not know how Burns left, only from his own statement.

It being here proposed to put in the statements of the prisoner since his arrest, Mr. Ellis called the attention of the court to the sixth section of the law, which provides that the evidence of the alleged fugitive shall not be taken. He therefore objected against such evidence being received.

Mr. Thomas, for the claimant, replied that Burns' admissions and confessions were a very different thing from testimony, he not being privileged to testify, as he was a party in the suit — the defendant.

Mr. Dana responded, sustaining the point of his associate. He regarded it as the height of cruelty to the prisoner to take advantage of the only power he had under this law, that of speech, to his detriment, when the claimant, the other party in the suit, had not only his own rights, but, in these alleged confessions, a portion of the prisoner's.

The court thought that the word "testimony," in the law, must be regarded as referring to evidence given by a witness, and not to confessions or admissions; but, nevertheless, he was unwilling to prejudice the liberty of the prisoner, and his counsel might have the right to pass that question for the present.

Mr. Parker asked that the questions might be asked, and the answers taken down for future use, if necessary.

The court assented and admitted *de bene.* Mr. Brent then proceeded : —

Burns said he did not intend to run away, but, being at work on board a vessel, and getting tired, fell asleep, when the vessel sailed with him on board. On Mr. Suttle's going into the room after the arrest, the first word from Burns was, " How do you do, Master Charles ? " The next thing was, " Did I ever whip you, Anthony ? " The answer was, " No." The next question, " Did I ever hire you where you did not want to go ? " The reply was, " No." The next question, " Did you ever ask me for money when it was not given you ? " The answer was, " No." Mr. Suttle then asked, " Did I not, when you were sick, take my bed from my own house for you ? " and the answer was, " Yes." He then recognized witness, (Brent,) and said, " How do you do, Master William ? "

Being asked substantially if he was willing to go back, he said he was. Burns' mother lived with Colonel Suttle, and is now on his place ; has a sister in Richmond, and a brother in Stafford county with Colonel Suttle ; knew of no fact, other than Burns' mother living on Suttle's farm, that she was his slave.

[The witness here found difficulty in explaining the relation of Suttle's alleged property to him, from the fact that the Court said he must not state any person to be "a slave" without corroborative legal evidence. Sundry questions bearing upon this point, were discussed at length by counsel.]

Brent continued.—When I hired Burns, I gave my bond to Suttle, who claimed to own. him ; on another occasion, when Col. Suttle was desirous of making some pecuniary transactions, he gave a mortgage on his property, including this man Burns, in order to raise the money ; he then stated that Burns was one of his slaves ; when he sent Burns to Richmond, to be hired out, he described him as his "boy ;" it is customary in Virginia, to give passes to slaves, when they go about, one of which Burns had when he came to his (witness') house in Richmond.

Cross Examined. — By Mr. Ellis. — I am 35 years of age ; lived always in Richmond ; am in the grocery commission business ; own slaves myself — acquired some by marriage 13 years ago, and became interested in others by my father's death in 1848 ; have bought some — the last in 1841 or 1842 ; never sold any myself ; further than that never traded in slaves. I came on with Col. Suttle, meeting him in Alexandria, twenty miles from my residence. I left Richmond Saturday week, morning, reached Alexandria same evening, and left at same time, coming as direct to Boston as facilities would allow ; had arranged beforehand with Suttle, that I should come on with him, the boat stopping at Alexandria for him to get on board ; he had said nothing about paying my expenses or remunerating me for coming ; came on with him, a volunteer, as a friend ; never went before on any similar expedition ; had accompanied him to Washington frequently as a friend, but never on any matter of an alleged runaway ; Col. Suttle first sent to me about coming on here ; I received a letter from him two or three days before coming on, in relation to it ; have never in any form communicated with him relative to coming on, and there has been no word or writing between us relative to any compensation ; we lodge and room together here, arriving here on Monday night last ; Tuesday after Burns was missing, I wrote to Suttle of the fact ; the man who hired him was named Millspaugh, his term of service commencing on the first of January last: the mortgage already alluded to was in the name of John M. Tolson, of Stafford County, Virginia ; the conversation with Burns since his arrest, occurred in the Marshal's room, in this building, in the presence of several police officers, between 8 1-2 and 8 o'clock on Wednesday night ; do not think he had irons on ; I have seen him with irons on ; the conversation commenced immediately after the remark from Burns, "How do you do, master Charles ?" Col. Suttle did say, "I make you no promises and I make you no threats ;" Suttle also said he would make no compromises with him ; heard nothing of any remark by Suttle, as to Burns better consenting to go back ; this is substantially the whole conversation ; was in the room some five minutes ; went there from the Revere, and then returned ; the reply of Suttle about promises and threats, and making no compromises, was after Burns said something about going back ; I have lived in Richmond four years ; Suttle resided in Alexandria two years ; went there two years ago next August ; before I came to Richmond, I lived in Stafford County, where also did Suttle, before he went to Alexandria.

By Mr. Dana. — Burns' mother lives at Stafford ; he has a brother and sister ; don't know that the bond between me and Suttle, as to the hiring of Anthony, is in existence ; am not responsible for Anthony's connection with Millspaugh, other than as agent, and which ceased when he escaped ; the conversation in the Marshal's room was not in the very words I have given, being categorically ; I only answer here the questions put to me ; and have stated the conversation as nearly as I can recollect. Burns' so-called mother was generally reputed to be such.

Caleb Page sworn. — Reside in Somerville; am a teamster; was present at the conversation alluded to with Burns in the Marshal's room: did not hear the first of the conversation, but remembered the questions relative to the giving of money, flogging, the use of the bed when sick, &c. Col. Suttle asked Anthony why he left him, or why he ran away, he did not remember which: he did not hear the answer, not being very near: Suttle asked him if he did not come in Captain Snow's vessel; Burns replied that he did not; he then asked what vessel he did come in, but witness did not hear the reply.

Cross-Examined. — By Mr. Ellis. — Am a teamster, in Milk street, working for various firms; own my own team; am not an officer; was asked to come and assist in arresting a man by Mr. Butman, he saying, " You are just the man I want; " I came to the court house with the prisoner; staid three-quarters of an hour; was not here all night, that night; I walked behind at the arrest; there were four men besides myself; the room where he was put is the same in which he has been confined; I am still employed in the case by the Marshal, have no written agreement, only his word of engagement; am employed as — [witness did not conclude the remark.]

Q. — How came Butman to say you were just the man ?

Mr. Parker. — You need not answer.

No response.

Mr. Parker then proposed to put in the record of the Court in Virginia, as evidence.

The Court said it was in the case subject to objection from counsel.

The counsel for the defence, after examining this record, said he should have several objections to present against it, which he should like to present to the Court in the absence of a jury.

Mr. Parker said the record was decisive of two points — 1st, that Anthony Burns owes service and labor; and 2d, that he had escaped, — and requested the Commissioner to examine in the manner most agreeable to himself the marks upon the prisoner, to see if they were at variance with those described in the document, to prove the identity.

The Court said he perceived the scars on the cheek and hand, and took cognizance with his eye of the height of the prisoner. " If the counsel wish, I will have him brought to me for further examination."

Mr. Ellis. — No; we only want all the evidence now put in that may be offered by the claimant to close the case.

Mr. Thomas for the claimant, cited the laws and authorities of Virginia relative to the organization and power of the Courts, and of the particular Court whose record has been adduced.

Mr. Dana. — A book is here presented to show that a person " owes service and labor " in Virginia. We deny the sufficiency of the evidence.

Mr. Thomas. — The proper way to prove the law of another State, is by books, as has been decided by our Supreme Court in 4 Pickering.

Mr. Ellis. — Saving exceptions, we are willing to close the case.

Mr. Thomas. — If the book is not sufficient, I wish to prove the fact in another way.

The Commissioner ruled the book in, admitting it as testimony, to go for what it would.

Messrs. Ellis and Dana asked for delay, that they may confer together relative to the defence, the qualification of some expected witnesses, and the examination of authorities alluded to.

The Court said (at 10 minutes to 3) he would allow a delay to half-past 3 o'clock.

A recess accordingly took place.

MR. ELLIS'S OPENING ARGUMENT.

MR. COMMISSIONER.

We wish for reasonable delay to prepare for the defence. We need time The prisoner needs it, and has reason for it. But, understanding the nature of these proceedings, we can only be thankful for the little that we have had at your hands. We too, sir, wish to see an end of what we witness, and we shall go on though utterly unprepared for such an issue, and, after stating the defence to the claim, shall produce such evidence as, in the very brief period that has passed, could be summoned. I trust, sir, if the case of the claimant as presented can commend itself to you as just in law and fact — when viewed alone, we have proof enough not only to make you pause, but to show you that the case is a claim not to be supported by you now.

Sir, of the very brief time granted, but a day in a case to decide more than that man's life, when, if it involved only his coat, the wheels of justice could not be turned in months, — most has not been available. This case involves novel questions of law, but the library has been locked up. Access to this house has been difficult. The Sabbath made part of the time. It is now next to impossible even for counsel to enter the Court Room, through the military forces. The common avenues are entirely barred and impassable. The labor and fatigue of a hurried preparation have been thus multiplied. Precious as every instant is to one needing to use it to defend another's liberty, I have to-day lost most of the few minutes pause, forbidden to ascend the stairway, by soldiers with their bayonets at my breast. Still, sir, we must go on.

We shall offer evidence to contradict that produced by the claimant, evidence upon the *facts* in issue.

But, before stating that, or appealing to it, we claim that here is no evidence offered that will warrant the signing the warrant of slavery.

We stand on the presumption, of which your Honor did well to remind counsel, of freedom and innocence.

We claim, not more from the instinctive feeling of common fairness and humanity, than from the just application of the plain principles of justice and law, that, in a case of this sort, that presumption applies with multiplied force and is to be held to most sacredly.

Sir, you sit here, judge and jury, betwixt that man and slavery. Without a commission, without any accountability, without any right of challenge, you sit to render a judgment which if against him no tribunal can review and no court reverse. He may be dragged before you without any warrant; you must proceed without any delay; without any charge, on proofs defined only as such as may satisfy your mind, you may adjudge, and your judgment to surrender will be final forever. Therefore, the proposition will commend itself to your Honor's reason and justice. The mind that is to decide a matter involving questions of law and of fact will not fail to weigh all these questions with the greater care the greater the chances of error and the dangers of its result, and, in this case, require the claimant to prove his case beyond a possible doubt.

Before proceeding with our evidence or stating it, we submit that, on their own showing, they have no case. They offer a paper which they call a record, one witness, and a book they call the laws of Virginia. On this we contend they have no claim to a certificate. This is one defence. We shall show it to be a good one. I design for a time to hold up to view such a case as they venture to present, before proceeding to our answer.

But when on Saturday morning we asked for delay of a day or two to prepare for the defence, the counsel of the claimant, against this presumption, and against his right, dared to say that we have no defence to make; and to-day, beginning as we do at the earliest hour on Monday, after less than a day available for labor, really gathering our facts as they are putting in their case, the counsel ventures again to hint the same thing. By what right? By what warrant? On what sort of presumption?

Sir, before proceeding to state the rules of law by which you are to judge this case, I am happy to be able to state that we shall offer proof that this atrocious charge, and seizure made on a false pretence of robbery, have no foundation in fact.

The slave claimant's attorney said, too, that we had no defence to the case but against the law; and that we came here to ask that that should be overridden, and the constitution violated. This too is not true. Not only have I never opposed the law, but I have done something to stay resistance to it. I stand here for the prisoner, under and not against the law. I shall not shrink from debating the just limits of this Bill of 1850. I trust I shall never fear to avow my utter hatred, as a man and a lawyer, of this Bill. But, in reply to this remark, and as a fit suggestion in approaching the debate, I will say, especially do I feel called upon to say, with these surroundings, with this form of seizure, charge, and procedure, in the midst of this Court House occupied like a fortress, filled with troops, every entrance guarded on every step, even counsel denied entrance for a long time, in a cause in which claims are asserted and advocated by armed men, held in a room, packed, in the main *packed*, in a proceeding in which the sole law officer of the general government dared to make the exhibition we have witnessed, that if there be any who do need especially to be reminded that there is a constitution and that there are laws, they are not the counsel for the prisoner. It is not I.

Please your Honor, I cannot consent that the counsel for the claimant, as Mr. Thomas thought to do, shall hint to me the line of my duty. I judge not of his course. I notice these things only because of his own provoking. I neither commend nor condemn their action. Their own consciences shall judge them. One, all of course expected to see here. The gentleman who for the first time appears in such a case, and whom it has been my privilege to call a friend, I did not think of meeting. But for myself, I do say, that sooner than lay my hand to the work of aiding in such a case I would see it wither, and rather than speak one word for a slave claimant I would be struck dumb forever.

It is my duty to remark, and I am led to do so more particularly because of the suggestion that we seek not a trial under but a triumph over the law, upon the real posture of the parties and the court. It is highly proper always that the mind, whether on the bench or in the jury box, which is to judge of fact or law, should perceive clearly every thing in the position of the parties, the form of procedure, the circumstances surrounding, and the results to follow, that may tend at all to disturb its balance. We stand here, you are here, sir, without a single one of the countless provisions with which the law so carefully surrounds every tribunal that is to sit in judgment, according to its position, for the preservation of its purity and the protection of innocence.

I cannot approach this case without being oppressed with the feeling that, not speaking merely with regard to the Slave Bill, but in view of the peculiar facts of this case, in almost every thing save the one thing wherein our hopes are centred,— your honor's judgment,—there is not to be found the image of a thing that can bear the shadow of the name of a trial. May not that mind fail in the coming ruin! *Inter arma leges silent.*

I shall have the honor to submit that some of the few decisions on this Bill on which the claimant relies as authority for this case were influenced by peculiar political views applied to this recent statute, which have no force remaining to support them as authorities, whilst otherwise are to be plainly distinguished from this, as most of them are. I now remark that this trial is political. It is strange that whilst our ears are insulted by guns for the passage of a new law to extend the area of the compromise, this trial is started here, and several others at the same moment in other distant places. That the learned District Attorney for the United States should have dared to rise here this morning, disobey the court, and overawe it, is more than strange. By and by, I shall say it is strange that they call on courts, relying on the faith of treaties which they have trampled on.

I approach this case thus because I must pass by these heaps of rubbish to reach it, because it is my right and my duty as a lawyer plainly to point out and to speak of every element in the law that may bear on your construction or administration of it, and those circumstances that may mislead, prejudice, or disturb you, and because I think that by this you will feel that we have the better right to fall back in confidence on your resistance to all. In but one thing, sir, in your narrow power of satisfying your mind on the narrowest points, in this alone is left the semblance of justice.

I choose, therefore, to dwell for a moment on all this. Seized on a false charge, without counsel, the prisoner is to be doomed. And then with no power to test jurisdiction, when every one of the writs of the common law for personal liberty's security is found to have failed, without time, without food, without free access to the court, without the show of free thought or action within it, without challenge for favor, or bias, for cause or without cause, without jury, without proofs, in form, or witnesses to confront him, with a judge, sitting with his hands tied, in nearly all points the merest tool of the most monstrous of anomalies, with no power to render a judgment, but full power to doom to the direst sentence, I say that, in all things, save one, in your opinion, the Prisoner has not the semblance of justice.

Clothed as you are with such transcendent powers, you must feel, and sir we are thankful to have this case before your honor, rather than — before your honor, because we do feel that however, whilst holding a post, you feel bound to do its duties, you will, in the exercise of this power to which the world can furnish no parallel, see to it that there can be no error possible, but you judge as you would be judged. Apart from this the Prisoner can have no hope. I choose, therefore, before turning to the light, before pointing out the way of escape, to see if any light can be thrown into this mass of blackness that is offered, to confront their case. I wish to look the men in the eye who dare to come here with pistols in their pockets, to ask us to meet a case with our opposing counsel armed, hemmed in with armed men, entering court with muskets at our breasts, trying a case under the muzzles of their guns. I choose to ask these men, face to face, by what show of right they speak of law and justice. All this is legitimate. It is worth considering. It will be remembered. I leave it.

Sir, it was and will be urged that this examination is preliminary. My learned associate well replied "To what?" Surely it is well to settle the preliminaries, and not to dwell on unimportant formularies. The examination in Virginia I suppose was preliminary. So shall each lay this to his soul who acts at any stage. Preliminary, sir, they know better when they say so. The law looks no further, nothing is to follow. There is no *postliminium*. This is the final act in the farce of hearings. They know, we know, you know, that if you send him hence with them, he goes to the block, to the sugar or cotton plantation, to the lash under which I have heard Sims, who entered the dark portal, breathed out his life, and that man is a fool who expects me to believe otherwise.

Therefore unless a case of overwhelming proof is presented, unless by no possibility could any but the slave of Suttle be seized or surrendered, is this certificate to be refused.

They call one witness; and, as additional evidence, produce a written paper which they call a record — to prove the facts of service, escape, and identity under the 6th section of the Bill of 1850. We claim that it is, on their own showing, a possible hypothesis, as we shall offer evidence to prove to your honor, that at the time of the alleged escape the person charged was a free man at work in Massachusetts.

1. This is admissible only under section sixth.

2. Being not a judicial tribunal, this magistracy can take no cognizance of the laws of all the States, now thirty and soon to be many more. Slavery or no slavery is always a complex question, of extreme nicety often.

3. The statutes of Virginia are not proved. There is reason why a judge in his circuit should be presumed to know them. The statutes of some States provide that the volumes printed by authority shall be taken in courts as *prima facie* proof. But there is no such law for this. These laws, therefore, must be proved as facts.

4. So too, must the existence and seal of the court. True, that being exhibited, binds you. But that must be proved. 1 *Greenleaf evidence.*

5. If this offered under *Constitution Art.* 4, § 1, as a record and its effect is to be tried by that provision and in the provision of the law tested by that, it must fail for the reason I will state. But it is not so offered because they cannot venture to assert that the act of the Virginia court or your honor's is judicial or this a judicial record at all.

6. No, this stands like the rest, or falls, under the protection of the clause for surrender of servants claimed, and the precise question arises on this, a constitutional question, though only on a point of evidence, can Congress as incident to the power of surrender, provide for a species of proof which so violates the principles of our laws and its own provisions. Especially consider article 4, § 2 of the Amendments, especially *art.* 5.

7. But the statute describes it as a record, and as such it is offered, and as such it is unconstitutional to make it evidence, because under art. 4, § 1, of the Constitution, the effect to be given to real records is limited. It is "full," no fuller than they have within the jurisdiction wherein they are made, and there no one would be bound without notice. 7 Metc. 333, *Gleason* v. *Dodd.* 1 Cush. 24, *Ewer* v. *Coffin.*

Again this record is not admissible, because it is not entire. It has no charge, no issue, no finding set forth.

2. It is not a copy of, but a transcript from the record, and so purports to be.

3. It is not a record "of the matters proved," it does not "certify the proof" as the Bill of 1850 provides in § 6.

4. It does not describe the prisoner with convenient certainty.

The complaint and warrant are illegal. They choose these rather than simple seizure, and unless this procedure knows no law, and follows no law, if they are to go by due process of law, they fail.

1. Neither the complaint nor warrant allege the fact of escape sufficiently. It is on or about a certain day.

2. There is no allegation sufficient as to the facts of service, how he is held, whether as apprentice or slave, by one as owner or as lessee, for life or years, to enable him to prepare a defence.

3. Nothing is prayed for that you can grant. The prayer is that you restore the prisoner to Suttle in Virginia. You cannot. Section 6 authorizes you to certify and him to take, and § 10 only authorizes you to deliver up. True they ask for other relief, but this not as is said of the prayer for general relief in Courts of Equity at all next to the Lord's prayer.

4. There is no description with convenient certainty.

1. The nature of the evidence offered is not sufficient, assuming all they offer it is this, that within a few years, the prisoner, rendering no acts of service to the claimant, only by hearsay said to have been born of a mother, also not shown to have rendered any service to Suttle, has been said by Suttle to belong to him. This is not sufficient. 1 Curtis 43, Morris' case, and cases cited there. *J. B. Monroe.*

2. Again admissions made by one claimed to be a slave are not admissible on the trial of freedom. 1 Green. ev. § 215, 220. *State* v. *Charity*, 214.

All confessions are to be excluded. "The master has an almost unlimited control over the body and mind of his slave. The master's will is the slave's will. All his acts, all his sayings are made with a view to propitiate his master. His confessions are made, not from a love of truth, not from a sense of duty, not to speak a falsehood but to please his master, and it is in vain that his master tells him to speak the truth and conceals from him how he wishes the question answered. The slave will ascertain, or which is the same thing, think that he has ascertained, the wishes of his master and moulds his answer accordingly. We therefore more often get the wishes of the master, or the slave's belief of his wishes, than the truth. And this is so often the case that the public justice of the country requires that they should be altogether excluded." *State* v. *Charity.*

Such is the law as laid down by the court of a slave state, in a trial there.

Need one pause to remark with what multiplied force the principles thus stated apply here to such a case as this.

3. The bill of 1850 itself in § 6 expressly provides that the testimony of the person claimed shall not be taken.

4. Surely if any circumstances should exclude this, these are enough.

Whatever rules you may choose to adopt in this case, whether in relation to your own powers, the construction of the statute, the admission or the weight of evidence, they ought to be such that it would not be possible for a man actually free, one of our own citizens to be hustled off, sacrificed under the fall of the presumptions under which the laws place him for protection. But under the rule asked for by the claimant, and sometimes adopted, under the claimant's case, if you should decide it for him, it would be perfectly possible that a man free as you or I should be taken. Let the marks of a free negro be noted, let him live here or in Richmond, let a record be made as this was, without notice to him or any one, let one witness state the fact of identity, and is there any chance for the truth to be established?

Does the fact of claim strengthen it? I supposed a case of one of our citizens. Suppose the prisoner lived in Richmond and was *claimed* there by Suttle in fact, but in fact free. You must adopt a rule to protect that right of freedom, in whatever form it is possible he or any one set to the bar might be entitled to it.

Therefore, I say, that by the law of Virginia, in establishing title on an issue of freedom, in case of one not born before 1785, it must be proved that there is direct descent from one then held as a slave, as well as continual ownership; and also that, not only by the law of Massachusetts but by the laws of all the states, by the law of Virginia, and by the constitution, no faith nor credit can be given to a record, which in any wise is to be used to impair one's person, estate, or liberty, unless it be proved that he was duly and fairly notified and bound to appear. Any other rule would be unjust, would open the door to obvious frauds, be destructive of liberty, deprive the citizens of the free states, as well as slaves, of their rights and immunities, and be a gross departure from the settled rules and maxims of the law.

We claim the utmost strictness of application of the settled rule of the common law as held in cases of murder, (and *a fortiori* here,) that the evidence must perfectly exclude any hypothesis but that claimed, and establish every fact beyond any reasonable doubt whatever. 1 Starkie ev. 5, 14, & *seq.*

1. We claim, too, that the amount of proof of one witness shall not be held enough. If it be, there can be safety for no man. It is true the common law *requires* but one witness in most cases. But this is *lege solutus.* Besides the law does require more in some cases. There are unanswerable reasons why in such a case as this, especially in this, more should be required.

2. In our law the amount of testimony goes, generally, to the jury.

The rule of Scripture is to be remembered, " One witness shall not rise up against a man for any iniquity. At the mouth of two or three witnesses shall the matter be established."

Such is the general law of other countries. Such is the general safe custom of juries in our own.

The reason of the rule "*unius responsio non audiatur*" is the fit rule for this case, "quia unus sibi facile constare possit."

But if this evidence be taken it must be all taken and the prisoner is free.

1. He is a mortgaged chattel. The mortgagee has the legal title, and is owner, and can alone reclaim. 10 Metcalf, 243, *Appleton* v. *Bancroft*, and 3 Cushing, 322, *Holmes* v. *Bell*, settled that a mortgagor, even if beneficially interested could neither maintain trover for the goods mortgaged, nor assumpsit for their proceeds.

2. He is leased; and if the right of reclamation depends on the present right of possession, the lessee alone can have that. The Bill of 1850 only authorizes the person holding, the person to whom the service is due, to reclaim; therefore the lessee is the one to recover. *George* v. *Eliot*, 152.

3. The evidence proves that there was no escape.

(a.) The constitutional power is limited to persons "escaping from service."

(b.) The statute is confined to cases of escape.

(c.) Now they choose to show that the prisoner fell asleep on board a vessel in the bay in a slave state, and a breeze came to waft him away out on to the high seas and into the safe port of a free state. It was a boon to him. It made him free. He finds himself here without escaping.

(d.) No act is to be done. He is free. He has gained something, but not illegally. The master has lost, but that is his fault, in not being a better keeper.

(e.) This is the general law of nations.

(f.) This is the law of the United States, and the provision applies only strictly to *casus fœderis*. In *Commonwealth* v. *Ames*, 18 Pick, and the case of the purser of the navy, so settled the law.

1. I come now to remark upon the Bill itself. On this point, too, I shall merely state my positions.

2. The counsel remarked that your honor is bound by numerous decisions; that all the judges of the circuits and districts, and many of those before whom it had come, and many commissioners had sustained this Slave Bill as a valid law.

I do not deny that there are decisions in its favor. I know them however to be far fewer in number than they suppose. But, sir, they cannot justly be said to be judicially obligatory on your action, closing this as *res adjudicata*. You are subordinate to no power whatever. The law has not been settled for you. Your decision upon the law is never to be drawn in question.

Nor has this broad question been reviewed by any court of highest resort in such form as to stand as authority over you save so far as it may commend itself to your judicial judgment.

4. In the first place this statute is a very recent one, only four years old, hardly yet trusted alone out of doors. No way is provided, but every possible way is contrived to prevent taking the judicial decision of any tribunal in the land upon it, save so far as the question may be incidentally involved in other cases, but each case must stand by itself before its own magistrate.

5. Again there are several classes of cases, and by far the largest part of all that have arisen, which are not of authority, to sustain this law, though they are often said to do so. One class is of those which only held a law on this subject to be constitutional, all they can or do decide is that under the Constitution, Congress may pass a law for restoration of slaves. I do not deny it; they hold that as by the law of 1793 trial by jury is taken away on the hearing, therefore that feature does not invalidate this bill. But what they decide, as in Sims' case on habeas corpus in Massachusetts, is that the courts cannot take one from custody of an officer of the law held under warrant from an officer having jurisdiction of the matter. Some of them, because the State tribunals cannot interfere with the process of the United States, an objection of which every lawyer at once feels the

force, some because the only inquiry open to them is whether the warrant issues from one having jurisdiction, they having no more right to decide the whole to be void because some provisions of the Bill are unconstitutional, than to suppose that he will not respect the provisions of the Constitution as far as they do limit his action under the statute.

Many were disposed of on purely technical points: they stand not so much as cases decided for the Bill, as attempts of the bar any where in every form to secure the protection of those processes, for protection of human liberty which have always existed under British law.

6. A few stand as cases decided in point, with such weight as may attach to the character of the commissioner. Some of the opinions have been written and printed in the papers. But, I must say of these few, though I promise you to speak of all with terms of such respect as I cannot feel for some, they are political cases.

In this use of the word *political* I attach to it a very different meaning from that I designed it should bear as applied to the other proceedings, to the causes which originate and the powers that uphold these proceedings. To all of these belong the term political in its worst sense.

But to the authority of these as precedents I apply the term in a far different sense. With perfect respect for the tribunals whose decisions are presented to us, I must say that they were influenced by considerations besides purely legal ones; the rules of construction have been influenced by matters not of judicial cognizance, and by circumstances which, however just, however proper to be weighed, must always leave these open on questions of a mere legal character. I see well how four years since no man, no court could fail to consider that this Bill was presented not alone, that its claims to support were not of a legal character, but that this bill stood as part of a system of grants and concessions, the best to be attained, to be acted on with a view to the political relations not of the parties but of the country. Who could help feeling that the first question was one of peace?

Of course, sir, I do not say that a judicial authority on a statute is to be changed because all is changed now. Just the reverse. I say that any that was influenced by such considerations at all is to be scrutinized accordingly. And we cannot fail to notice what is stated distinctly in more than one opinion as the chief reason for recognizing this statute as a valid law, or valid in its chief provisions, and to remark of it that it is not a matter of legal cognizance at all in any form.

Lord Clarendon, himself a lawyer, said that in the cases of the ship-money the judges declared as law from the bench what every man in the hall knew not to be law.

I apply no such remark sweepingly to all cases. To many I know it is not just. Many of the cases a lawyer knows must have been decided as they were from reasons to which I have alluded, cases involving the question only collaterally, cases disposed of on different grounds. Many of the dicta in those cases, for us as well as against, must be forgotten.

But with due regard to this great fact, to the fact that this Bill is of such recent date, that there have been conflicting decisions and dicta upon it and on various parts of it, that the least that can be said is that the sense of the bar as well as of the country is divided, this can hardly be held to be a matter settled by conclusive judicial precedent.

If it be not too late, it is fit to apply the maxim, *melius recurrere quam male currere.*

7. It is to be noted that this Bill has been sustained on the authority of the law of 1793. That reason has had weight to which the facts give it no claim. It is true, that the existence of the law of 1793 upon the statute book is a just legal reason for recognizing this bill, in so far as it involves no new principles, as a valid law. But no farther.

Let it be admitted then, for this debate, that the law of 1793 was constitutional, that that did not provide for a trial by jury. Still not a step is taken in the argument that would sustain this bill. This bill has new features, and what they are we see and feel, and how momentous they are is best to be judged from the fact that they were pressed, even to the hazard of peace, to the statute book and are to be forced, in spite of every consideration whatsoever, to judgment.

The law of 1793 did not provide for trial by jury, it is true, but it did not prevent it. That set one man to judge, but it did not prevent him from a judgment on the rules of evidence and the facts in the case. This presents to you a paper for which no one is responsible, blinds your eyes to the truth, although it has not yet been judicially settled, says you shall not inquire into it, says you must try, but summarily, and ties your hands to a single act.

8. That law, too, left the issue in such a position, that if the party chose he could have his trial secured before the magistrate and secured elsewhere. This, cuts off any legal process. The writ *de homine replegiando*, which we had thought to be part of the common law, to be matter of common right, to exist under the act of 1789, is held to have no longer any existence. The habeas corpus is suspended. Coke would think all this required a new Petition of Rights. He might have thought that such a sacrifice of rights, even in this anomalous procedure, could be withstood on the hallowed principles of the English law, and defended against under the constitution of the country.

This Bill goes beyond the statute of 1793 in the mode of instituting, the time of prosecuting, the mode of proving, the mode of conducting the trial, and the mode of enforcing the decision.

I will now state briefly the positions on which, if you do not feel bound to execute this as a settled law in all its details, I claim that this bill of 1850 ought to be declared to be unconstitutional.

9. It undertakes to give to the Virginia court judicial power.

10. It gives to a record of the Virginia court an effect not warranted by the constitution.

11. If the paper offered be viewed as evidence merely, the constitution nowhere gives any power to make any such proofs.

Art. 3, Sec. 1 has been considered, and, of course, cannot confer it.

It cannot exist as incident to the power of reclamation, because however anomalous in form, that is limited by the rights of citizens, as declared in the provisions presently to be referred to.

12. It confers judicial power on you. This position has never been answered; the knot is only cut.

Justly analyzed, all the objections to this that I have heard, do not relate to your function. It cannot be denied that all the essential elements of a judgment are involved in it. They all relate, not to the powers you possess, but to the form of their exercise. In such a view, I agree this is not a judicial proceeding.

13. It not only does not secure trial by jury as the act of 1793 did not, but it practically prevents the possibility of securing it or of resorting to any form of process for relief.

14. It violates the provision of article 4 of the Amendments, which guaranties persons against unreasonable seizures.

15. It violates that of article 5, that no one shall be deprived of liberty without due process of law, and also articles 6 and 7.

16. This is not a power that is delegated to Congress.

17. It goes to defeat the intent of the constitution, and is contrary to the spirit of our laws.

For these reasons the claimant shows no claim to a certificate; but the charge of escape is not true. The title is not his; he ought not to have his claim allowed.

If such a case stood alone, we feel that it ought to be dismissed.

But the prisoner has an answer to it, a case of his own. It can be stated in a word. The complaint alleges, the record offered only proves, the only witness called testifies to an escape on the twenty-fourth day of March last, from Richmond. The witness swears clearly and positively that he saw this prisoner in Richmond on the nineteenth day of March.

We shall call a number of witnesses to show, fixing as I think the man and the time beyond question, that the prisoner was in Boston on the first of March last, and has been here ever since up to the time of this seizure.

This is our defence. Thus do we answer the case of the claimant, and hold that it must be tried by these rules. Yet I feel that in these cases no one knows what ground he stands upon.

Common justice, therefore, demands that you give us the benefit of every doubt on the questions of law, and on the issues of fact.

You will, I know, not consider me as expressing the slightest want of confidence or disrespect. I say frankly and publicly, I am glad this case is not before others. But, sir, we know not whom to trust. Who knows that he can trust himself? What influences may be about you—what may be your opinions I know not. But this I do feel, to the peril of the prisoner, that a man must be more than mortal if he can close his eyes and ears to a thousand things that reach them where you sit, all aimed at the destruction of the prisoner.

Be sure, therefore, that you make no error in your law. Be sure that your reason and judgment are beyond all danger of bias. Be sure that you make no mistake in fact, for you sit in judgment on this cause, with powers such as are no where else intrusted to mortal man in the civilized world, and your responsibilities correspond to them.

In our courts, a criminal has the benefit of every error in law, and the benefit of every doubt, with the jury. The prisoner at the bar can rightly, because of your unlimited powers, claim of you, as a matter of honor and magnanimity, the most liberal measure of fairness that he could ever ask at the hands of court or jury, and demand of you to see that you justly give to him all he could secure at their hands by any form of legal protection.

EVIDENCE FOR THE DEFENCE.

The witnesses for the defence were then called. The first was—

William Jones (colored): Reside in South Boston; am a laborer; know Burns; saw him first on Washington street the first day of March; I talked with him half an hour; I employed him to go to work on the 4th day of March in the Mattapan works at South Boston; worked at cleaning windows; he worked with me there five days; the day I saw him I made a minute of it in Mr. Russell's shop and asked Mr. Russell to put it down on my book; keep a memorandum; can't write myself; the entries were made in the book by Mr. Russell; I agreed to give him eight cents a window, and when he got through with the windows, I gave him a dollar and a half; he said I hadn't settled up with him right; he went to the clerk about it; I have that memorandum book; (it was handed to the counsel); on referring to this book I am able to state that I did go with him at this time to South Boston to work.

Cross-examined.—Never saw Burns before I saw him on Washington street; he spoke to me first; don't recollect the day of the week; about the first of the week; I saw him just below the *Commonwealth* office; he was alone; it was between eleven and twelve o'clock; he had on lightish pants; can't describe his dress more particularly because it wasn't my business to examine his dress;

he had on a lightish coat and cap; he asked me if I knew of any one that wanted a man to work in a store; I said, What can you do? he said he could do most any thing; I took him from there to Mr. Russell's shop, and went from there to Mr. Favor's shop; Russell keeps in the next street to Water street; don't know his Christian name; he keeps a boot black shop; stayed there five minutes; went from there to Mr. Favor's in Lincoln street and stayed there three quarters of an hour; then to an apothecary shop under the U. S. Hotel; I went there to fool; I fetched up there; I don't know what Burns went for; I stayed there twenty-five or thirty minutes; I next went to Mr. Maddox's in Essex street; he keeps a clothing store; arrived there about two o'clock; had nothing else to do but walk round the city; after leaving Maddox's came down Washington street; went into Mr. Bell's, dancing master; he went there with me; didn't remain half a second for he wan't in; then went down Washington to Kneeland street, and then went home at South Boston; Burns went with me; it was night when we arrived home; I had not dined; I eat but one meal a day, and have no particular hour for that; it was a little cold; there might have been snow on the ground, but I don't recollect; don't recollect whether it snowed or rained; it might have rained twenty times and I not notice it; he stayed with me that night, the next night, and the next, and the next; I never expected to see this that I see here now; the next morning after he went home with me, he came to the City Hall to see Mr. Gould; don't know his Christian name; I went to see if there were any orders; it was between ten and eleven o'clock; went to get employment for myself; next went to School street; then went out on the Neck to take a walk and see what I could see; didn't call on any body but Mr. Gould; next day got up, washed my face and hands; went to the Mattapan Works; saw Mr. Sawyer, the boss; stayed two or three hours; talked with him about the job; went home about eleven or twelve; Burns' was with me all the time; went back to the Mattapan Works and commenced work at one o'clock; remained there till night; Burns was with me all the time; he helped me clean the windows; next morning went back to work with me; he had no trunk; worked all day; next day cleaned windows; never keep the run of the weather, or the day of the week; after finishing my work at the Mattapan Works went to City Hall to see Mr. Gould; Burns went with me; there was no work to be done and we went home then; on the 18th day of March went to work at City Hall; he was with me there about three times; he made fire under the boiler for me as an accommodation; he stayed with me until the 18th; I left him here on the morning of 18th; never put eyes on him again until Sunday morning, when I saw him looking out of the window of the Court House; I stood on the opposite side; his head was out of the window; it was near twelve o'clock; had been before to the Revere House and called on Col. Suttle; went on the Friday previous to see Suttle; it was Thursday or Friday; saw a good many men besides Suttle; didn't know any of them; had never seen Colonel Suttle any where else; might have seen him in Virginia, but I didn't know him; first heard of the arrest of Burns on Thursday; came into the Police Court and the Municipal Court; I heard there was a man arrested and I walked round here and I didn't believe; one of the officers told me of the arrest; I stayed at the Court House all night Friday night, me and a watchman together, protecting the city property; I employed myself; didn't come into the Court Saturday because I couldn't get in; nobody spoke to me about being a witness here; I came here because I saw this man looking out of the window; have had no conversation with any body about this matter until yesterday; I mentioned it to many; came here this morning with Mr. Lawton; went from this Court House at 7 1-2 o'clock Saturday night and came back as the bells were ringing for church Sunday morning, and went to the Revere House; was at the meeting in Faneuil Hall, and came from there when the meeting broke up; stood in Court street until the mob left the square, and then went up the square to protect the city property; first heard him called Anthony Burns on Thursday; a man read it from the newspaper; I called him John and Jack, or any short name that came handy; have not spoken to Mr. Carlton, an officer, since Friday or Saturday; spoke to Mr. Carlton in the Marshal's office; might have passed some words with him; didn't tell him that Burns belonged to Col. Suttle; applied to the Marshal for a permit to see Burns, and he said he wouldn't let his master see him; I didn't say if I saw him I would advise him to go back.

George H. Drew (white) called. Was book-keeper at the Mattapan Works until the 18th of this month. Knew that Jones was employed about the first of March to wash windows at the Mattapan Works; he was there several days; there were two or three men with him; there was a colored man working with him; had not seen the prisoner at the bar from the time he worked there until I saw him here yesterday; yesterday came in here and when I saw Burns recognized him; now recognize him; saw him before with Jones when Jones came to get a job, and I referred him to Mr. Sanger; I looked at this man and asked Jones if he was his brother, and he said, All men are my brothers; about the first of March, after I settled with Jones, Burns came to me and asked me how much I paid Jones; don't recollect the number of days they worked; have no doubt of the identity of the man; recognize him by his general appearance; saw him enough here to recognize him; when I came in yesterday, Burns followed me all round the room with his eyes; I paid Jones for his work.

Cross-examined. Saw him twice to notice him particularly; one of these times was when he came to ask how much I paid Jones; and the other when they came to see about the job; somebody sent for me yesterday noon, saying I might be wanted as a witness here; was brought here yesterday to look at Burns; Mr. Stetson came to me yesterday at my residence 13 Indiana place; I hadn't been here before yesterday; Stetson said I was wanted as a witness at the Court House; was outside of the Court House yesterday morning; was not outside of the Court House Friday or Friday night; was about here one hour on Saturday; I never noticed the scar on his hand.

The Court here adjourned to three o'clock.

AFTERNOON SESSION.

The hearing was resumed at quarter past three.

EVIDENCE FOR THE DEFENCE CONTINUED.

George W. Drew (re-called) testified that the way in which he fixed the day of Burns being at work at the Mattapan Works was by the entry in the cash book; I paid Jones $1,50 on the 4th of March, and made a final settlement with him on the 28th, paying him in all $33,50; the work had been finished some days when I settled with him; the first work he did was cleaning the windows.

James F. Whittemore sworn. — Reside in Boston; am a machinist; in March last was connected with the Mattapan Works; am a member of the City Council; went West some time in the first of March; returned the eighth of March; know the man at the bar; saw him on the morning of the 8th and 9th of March, at our shop at South Boston; he was cleaning windows with Mr. Jones [Burns stood up, and was recognized by the witness]; I then noticed the mark on his cheek, and also the mark on his right hand; have seen him in court to-day; when I saw him at the shop it was the first time I had been to the shop after my return, and I went immediately after my return.

Cross examined — Know it was the 8th of March when I returned because I left Philadelphia on the 6th; I called no attention to the marks at that time; when I first saw Burns he was on the outside; he remained outside a quarter of an hour; Mr. Drew was in the room at the time with others; the firm failed in the month of April; the first time after that that I saw Burns was this morning; I came in to see if I could identify him; no one asked me to come; something was said about his being the same man who was employed by Mr. Jones to clean windows; I knew that man and came in to see if it was him; I took my seat before looking at him; looked round and saw Burns and immediately stated to a person beside me that he was the man; I stated this to Mr. Putnam; the conversation I alluded to was held at the office of Mr. Ellis, this morning. I went to the office with Mr. Putnam; did not know what business he went there on; it was rumored that an attempt would be made to prove that Burns was here before the middle of March, and I supposed Mr. Putnam went in there in connection with that business; can't say from whom I heard this rumor; I heard it last evening at the armory of the military company to which I belong, the Pulaski Guards. I heard there that Mr. Jones employed the prisoner about the first of March; said nothing to any one about it; made up my mind I would come to see the prisoner; I was served with a notice this morning; was in Mr. Ellis's office when I was served with this notice; Mr. Jones was not there at that time; I saw him there a short time afterwards; had previous to this had no conversation with Jones about working at his shop with this colored man.

To Mr. Dana.— Am Lieutenant of the Pulaski Guards; have no particular interest in this case; do not lie under the imputation of being a Free Soiler or Abolitionist; I am a hunker Whig.

Stephen Maddox (colored) sworn — Live at 72 Essex street; keep a clothing store; kept there in March; know Burns; saw him at my store in March with Mr. Jones; it was about noon; he was there about five or ten minutes; I fix the time by Mr. Jones asking of me if I had any work; I stated that my outside work didn't commence for two months, the first of May, that is all I can fix the time by. I particularly noticed the mark on Burns' left cheek; I didn't see him again till I saw him to-day at 10 o'clock in this room; came in here with Mr. Jones, Russell, and others; I recognized him myself without his being pointed out to me.

Cross-Examined. — Have been at 72 Essex street since August last; before that was in Washington street, and carried on the same business; was not born here; did not ask his name when he called on me; Mr. Jones did not mention his name; the next time I saw Jones I said nothing to him about Burns; I think Burns had on lightish clothes when he called with Jones; don't know whether he had an overcoat on; can't say what I did the rest of the day; Mr. Jones said I was summoned to be here, on account of that man who came to my shop; I told him I would be here at 9 o'clock; came at 8 o'clock; came in with Jones between 9 and 10; have had no conversation with Mr. Jones about Burns, until he told me that I was summoned; talked about it two or three minutes; have not talked about it with Jones to-day; I spoke to Mr. Ellis about it this morning, in his office; Jones went there with me; I fix the time of Burns being in my shop by the fact that I told Mr. Jones that my busy time did not commence for two months, which would be the first of May; I mean by my outside work, cleaning windows, shaking carpets, &c.; came past the court house on Friday night, after the adjournment of the Faneuil Hall meeting; stayed about twenty minutes, then went home; did not see Jones that night; was about here half an hour on Saturday; was not here on Sunday.

William C. Culver sworn. Am a blacksmith; was employed by the Mattapan Company in March; recollect Mr. Jones and his men being there cleaning windows; it was prior to the time we changed our hours of work, which was the first of April.

John Favor. — Reside in Boston; am a carpenter; reside in Lincoln street; saw Jones in my shop in March; he had a colored man with him; he came to get employment for the colored man with him; didn't see the man who was with Jones again until yesterday; I thought I could recognize him if I saw him; when I came into court I recognized him as the man who came with Jones to my place, about the first of March; I have no doubt of it; it was between the first and fifth of March, I should think; have nothing by which I can fix the date definitely.

Cross-Examined. — When he came with Jones to my shop I conversed with him.

H. N. Gilman sworn. — Live in Boston; in March worked for the Mattapan Company; remember Jones's working there, and having a colored man with him; noticed a scar upon his face; I saw him after the work was finished in the counting room; the next time I saw him was in the court this morning; Mr. Jones asked me yesterday if I didn't recollect the man who was in his employ last spring; have since been summoned; Burns was not pointed out to me; I recognized him; he is the person who was at work for the Mattapan Company in March.

Cross-Examined. — Was a teamster for the Mattapan Iron Works; I saw Burns working there four or five days; perhaps half an hour in all; left their employ the 13th of April; we were paid off the first of the month, and it was near pay day that I saw him; I feel sure that it was done before the middle of March; I am more sure that it was the first week in March than that it was the second week.

Rufus A. Putnam sworn. — Am a machinist; was employed by the Mattapan Company in March; remember Jones and a colored man working there; fix the time by commencing a job at the time Jones was at work there, and also by the change of hours for commencing and ending work.

Cross-Examined. — Took the job the first part of March, and it was then that Jones was there; it was before the 10th of March; have memoranda which enables me to fix the time; I will swear that it was before the 6th of March that I commenced the job; commenced it before the 5th; I can swear it was before the 3d of March that I commenced the job; I went to Mr. Ellis's office this morning, by request of Mr. Drew; I went in with Mr. Whittemore; can't say whether I asked him to go in with me; was never in there before; looked at my memorandum on Sunday; I commenced the job just before Mr. Jones was there; the job is not done yet.

Horace W. Brown, (police officer). — Reside in South Boston; (Burns stood up); I have seen that man before; he was cleaning windows at the Mattapan Works, South Boston; I was at work there as carpenter; I left work there the 20th of March; saw Jones and Burns at work there some week or ten days before I left; I have not the slightest doubt about the man.

Cross-Examined. — My attention was first called to this matter this afternoon; never spoke to any one about it until I saw the prisoner this afternoon; I came here of my own accord; don't know who I first spoke to about it; told Dr. York that I had seen that man; have never seen him since he was at South Boston, until I saw him here; I heard a rumor that the man in court was the man who cleaned windows with Jones, and I came in to see if I should know him; worked for the Mattapan Company from April to the 20th of March; have seen no paper in which Jones's testimony given this forenoon was published; I left on the 20th of March; Burns was at work there about ten days before I left; Burns was at work on the windows; I called on Burns to clean a window where I was at work; I was paid $29 50 on the 3d of April; it was ten or twelve days after I quit work, before I was paid off; know Burns by his general appearance and by the scar on his face; thought I should know him by this mark; and said so to some of the men in the police office.

This ended the case for the defence.

REBUTTING EVIDENCE.

Several witnesses to rebut the testimony for the defence were then called.

Mr. Cyrus Gould sworn. — Did not hear Jones's testimony this morning; was about the City Hall the 18th of March; have charge of the building; was about it all the month of March; Jones worked there on the 10th two or three hours; he worked for me on the 16th and 17th of March; he was cleaning up; I did not see Burns with Johes there at any time; there was no man working with him; two women were working with him;-I employed Jones on this occasion; at the time I employed him he had these women with him.

—— Carlton. — Know Jones; have had conversation within a few days with Jones on the subject of which he testified to day; he came into the Marshal's office when I was there. [Inquiry was made as to conversation with Jones there, but Mr. Dana objected on the ground that Jones's testimony to the same conversation was ruled out this morning by objection of the claimant's counsel.] The Commissioner ruled that no conversation to which the claimants objected this morning could be admitted.

The Court then adjourned, to 9 o'clock this (Wednesday) morning.

Wednesday Morning, May 31st.

The hearing in the case of Burns was resumed this morning. There was even less excitement in and about the court house than there was yesterday. The only unusual appearance was the large military and civic guard which was on duty.

Among the spectators in court was Hon. Joshua R. Giddings, member of Congress from Ohio.

The Commissioner came in at 9 o'clock, and more rebutting evidence was introduced. The first called was

. Erastus B. Gould — Reside in Boston; have had care of the city building for two years; know Jones; I employed him to work for me on that building on the 26th of March; employed him at no other time in March; he had two women working with him; but no man; never saw Burns about the building; I am there only mornings and nights.

Cross-examined — My brother goes to the city building at morning and at night.

William R. Batchelder — Conversed with Mr. Jones Monday or Tuesday of this week; it was at the outside door of the court house, between six and seven o'clock, Monday night; [defence objected to what it was he said, and the court sustained the objection, on the ground that Jones was not inquired of as to the conversation.]

It was decided to recall Mr. Jones, and Mr. Batchelder's further examination was deferred until after Jones's reëxamination.

Benj. True — Have conversed with the defendant (Burns) within a day or two. [Counsel objected to the evidence. The counsel for the claimant proposed to show by this witness, by Burns' admission, that he came to Boston on the 19th of March. Mr. Dana objected that the admissions of the man under arrest should not be received at all. Again he objected because it was not rebutting testimony. The evidence introduced that Burns was here on the first of March was simply contradictory to the testimony for the claimant that Burns was in Virginia on the 20th of March, and they are now simply reinforcing their former testimony. Mr. Thomas (for the claimant) argued that the evidence alluded to by Mr. Brent was simply to prove the identity of Burns, and not to establish the fact of his being in Virginia on the 20th. The defence propose to prove an alibi, and we introduce this evidence to control their evidence sustaining the alibi.]

Mr. Dana renewed the objection, that it was simply contradictory evidence.

The Commissioner ruled that the testimony was admissible, but gave the counsel notice that if he changed his mind subsequently, before the arguments, he would inform them.

Witness resumed — This conversation was every day since he has been here; last Friday or Saturday had conversation with him about how long he had been here; it was up stairs in the place where he is kept; it was in the morning I think; I was there as Deputy Marshal in charge of Burns.

Mr. Ellis objected to the evidence on account of the relation which the witness bore to Burns; that confessions made to him were made under intimidation, and therefore should not be received. The evidence was admitted.

Witness resumed — Am a constable of Boston; first saw the prisoner on the night of his arrest; I was asked to go into the Marshal's office; Mr. Freeman said he wanted to use me; he told me to go up stairs to a room where there was a prisoner; I didn't know what the prisoner was there for until I got up stairs; found five or six men there; two of them are sitting beside him now; one is Mr. Pray; Mr. Butman was one; another was Moses G. Clark; Mr. Coolidge was there, and Mr. Page; my instructions were to stay there and see that no one came except by the direction of the Marshal; stayed there Wednesday night and have been there since; I was armed with a sword and pistol Friday night; these arms are kept in the rooms; there are six of us in the room; the Marshal and others came into the room Wednesday night; there was a good deal of talk between the officers and Burns; don't recollect any one saying he must go back; he first appeared terrified; been talking about Massachusetts, Virginia, and other matters; I never threatened him or held out any promises to him; we endeavored to treat him well; gave him newspapers, oranges, oyster stews and candy when he wished them; he can read and write.

Mr. Ellis objected, in view of this evidence, that the admissions of Burns should not be received, because it was established by it that they were not voluntary, but were given under circumstances which amounted to intimidation; and the whole circumstances since had been such as to increase his intimidation. Mr. Thomas argued that the ground of intimidation had not been made out, and the commissioner ruled that the evidence was admissible.

Witness resumed—The conversation was on Friday and Saturday; on Friday conversed with Burns about the length of time he had been here; he said he had been here about two months, perhaps a little short of that; said nothing else about the time he had been here; he said he had been in Richmond, Virginia, before that time.

With the close of the examination of this witness, the counsel for the claimants rested their case.

MR. DANA'S ARGUMENT.

I congratulate you, Sir, that your labors, so anxious and painful, are drawing to a close. I congratulate the commonwealth of Massachusetts, that at length, in due time, by leave of the Marshal of the United States and the District Attorney of the United States, first had and obtained therefor, her courts may be reopened, and her Judges, suitors and witnesses may pass and repass without being obliged to satisfy hirelings of the United States Marshal and bayoneted foreigners, clothed in the uniform of our army and navy, that they have a right to be there. I congratulate the city of Boston, that her peace here is no longer to be in danger. Yet I cannot but admit that while her peace here is in some danger, the peace of all other parts of the city has never been so safe as while the Marshal has had his posse of specials in this Court House. Why, Sir, people have not felt it necessary to lock their doors at night, the brothels are tenanted only by women; fighting dogs and racing horses have been unemployed, and Ann street and its alleys and cellars show signs of a coming millennium.

I congratulate, too, the Government of the United States, that its legal representative can return to his appropriate duties, and that his sedulous presence will no longer be needed here in a private civil suit, for the purpose of intimidation, a purpose which his effort the day before yesterday showed every desire to effect, which, although it did not influence this Court in the least, I deeply regret your Honor did not put down at once, and bring to bear upon him the judicial power of this tribunal. I congratulate the Marshal of the United States that the ordinary respectability of his character is no longer to be in danger from the character of the associates he is obliged to call about him. I congratulate the officers of the army and navy that they can be relieved from this service, which as gentlemen and soldiers surely they despise, and can draw off their non-commissioned officers and privates, both drunk and sober, from this fortified slave-pen, to the custody of the forts and fleets of our country, which have been left in peril, that this great Republic might add to its glories the trophies of one more captured slave.

I offer these congratulations in the belief that the decision of your Honor will restore to freedom this man, the prisoner at the bar, whom fraud and violence found a week ago a free man on the soil of Massachusetts. But rather than that your decision should consign him to perpetual bondage, I would say — let this session never break up! Let us sit here to the end of that man's life, or to the end of ours. But, assured that your Honor will carry through this trial, the presumption which you recognized in the outset, that this man is free until he is proved a slave, we look with confidence to a better termination.

Sir Matthew Hale said it was better that nine guilty men should escape than that one innocent man should suffer. This maxim has been approved by all jurists and statesmen from that day to this. It was applied to a case of murder, where one man's life was on one side and the interest of an entire community on the other. How much more should it be applied to a case like this, where on the one side is something dearer than life, and on the other no public interest whatever, but only the value of a few hundred pieces of silver, which the claimant himself, when offered to him, refused to receive. It is not by rhetoric, but in human nature, by the judgment of mankind, that liberty is dearer than life. Men of honor set their lives at a pin's fee on a point of etiquette. Men peril it for pleasure, for glory, for gain, for curiosity, and throw it away to escape poverty, disgrace, or despair. Men have sought for death, and digged for it as for hid treasure. But when do men seek for slavery, for captivity? I have never been one of those who think human life the highest thing. I believe there are things more sacred than life. Therefore I believe men may sacrifice their own lives, and the community, sometimes the single man, may take the lives of others. Such is the estimation in which it is held by all mankind. No! there are some in my sight now who care nothing for freedom, whose sympathies all go for despotism; but thank God they are few and growing less. Such is the estimate of life compared with freedom, which the common opinion of mankind and the common experience of mankind has placed upon it. Here is a question of a few despised pieces of silver on the one hand, and on the other perpetual bondage of a man, from early manhood to an early or late grave, and the bondage of the fruit of his body forever. We have a right, then, to expect from your Honor a strict adherence to the rule that this man is free until he is proved a slave beyond every reasonable doubt, every intelligent abiding misgiving proved by evidence of the strictest character, after a rigid compliance with every form of law which statute, usage, precedent has thrown about the accused as a protection.

We have before us a free man. Col. Suttle says there was a man in Virginia named Anthony Burns; that that man is a slave by the law of Virginia; that he is *his* slave, owing service and labor to *him*; that he escaped from Virginia into this State, and that the prisoner at the bar is that Anthony Burns. He says all this. Let him prove it *all!* Let him fail in one point, let him fall short the width of a spider's thread, in the proof of all his horrid category, and the man goes free.

Granted that all he says about his slave in Virginia be true — is this the man?

On the point of personal identity, the most frequent, the most extraordinary, the most notorious, and sometimes the most fatal mistakes have been made, in all ages. One of the earliest and most pathetic narratives of Holy Writ is that of the patriarch, cautious, anxious, crying again and again, "Art thou my very son Esau?" and by a fatal error, reversing a birth-right, with consequences to be felt to the end of time. You know, Sir — they are matters of common knowledge — that a mother has taken to her bosom a stranger for an only son, a few years absent at sea. Whole families and whole villages have been deceived and perplexed in the form and face of one they have known from a child. You have found it difficult to recognize your own classmates, at the age of three or four and twenty, who left you in their sophomore year. Brothers have mistaken brothers. We have the Comedy of Errors. Let us have no Tragedy of Errors, here! The first case under this statute, the case of Gibson, in Philadelphia, was a mistake. He was sworn to, and the commissioner was perfectly satisfied, and sent him to Maryland. Against the will of the claimant, from the humanity of the Marshal, who had his doubts, and would not leave the man at the State line, but went with him to the threshold of the door of the master's house, the mistake was discovered before it was too late. In the late case of Freeman, in Indiana, the claimant himself was present, and the testimony was entirely satisfactory, and he was remanded; but it turned out a mistake, and he has recovered, I am told, $2,000 in damages. These are the mistakes discovered. But who can tell over to you the undiscovered mistakes? the numbers who have been hurried off, by some accidental resemblance of scars or cuts, or height, and fallen as drops, undistinguishable, into the black ocean of slavery?

Make a mistake here, and it will probably be irremediable. The man they seek has never lived under Col. Suttle's roof since he was a boy. He has always been leased out. The man you send away would be sold. He would never see the light of a Virginia sun. He would be sold at the first block, to perish after his few years of unwonted service, on the cotton fields or sugar fields of Louisiana and Arkansas. Let us have, then, no chance for a mistake, no doubt, no misgiving!

What, then, is the evidence? They have but one witness, and one piece of paper. The paper cannot identify, and the proof of identity hangs on the testimony of one man. It all hangs by one thread. That man is Mr. Brent. Of him, neither you nor I, Sir, know anything. He tells us he is engaged in the grocery business, and lives in Richmond, Virginia. Beyond this, we know nothing, good or bad. He knew Burns when a boy, running about at Col. Suttle's, too young to labor. He next hired him himself, in 1846, and '7. This was seven years ago. He says Burns is now 23 or 24 years of age. He was then 16 or 17 years old; he is now a matured man.

Since that time he has leased him, as agent for Col. Suttle, but does not seem to have been brought in close contact with him, or to have done more than occasionally meet him in the streets. The record they bring here describes only a dark complexioned man. The prisoner at the bar is a full blooded negro. Dark complexions are not uncommon here, and more common in Virginia. The record does not show to which of the great primal divisions of the human race the fugitive belongs. It might as well have omitted the sex of the fugitive. It says he has a scar on one of his cheeks. The prisoner has, on his right cheek, a brand or burn nearly as wide as the palm of a man's hand. It says he has a scar on his right hand. A scar! The prisoner's right hand is broken, and a bone stands out from the back of it, a hump an inch high, and it hangs almost useless from the wrist, with a huge scar or gash covering half its surface. Now, Sir, this broken hand, this hump of bone in the midst, is the most noticeable thing possible in the identifying of a slave. His right hand is the chief property his master has in him. It is the chief point of observation and recollection. If that hand has lost its cunning or its power, no man hears it so soon and remembers it so well as the master. Now, it is extraordinary, Sir, that neither the record nor Mr. Brent say any thing about the most noticeable thing in the man. Nowhere in Mr. Brent's testimony does he allude to it, but only speaks of a cut. The truth is, please your Honor, one of two things is certain here. If Mr. Brent does know intimately Anthony Burns, of Richmond, and has described him as fully as he can, the prisoner is not the man. Anthony Burns was missing, and Mr. Brent hurried down to Alexandria to tell Col. Suttle. The record is made up, which is probably still only Mr. Brent on paper. Mr. Brent comes here with Col. Suttle, as his friend. Emissaries are sent out with the description in their hand, and they find a negro, with a huge brand on his cheek and a broken and cut hand, and that is near enough for catchers, paid by the job, to a "dark complexioned man," with "a scar on the cheek and on the right hand." Mr. Brent knows, and does not swear otherwise, that the Anthony Burns he means had only a scar or cut, and he distinctly said "no other mark." But still he swears to the man. Identification is matter of opinion. Opinion is influenced by the temper, and motive, and frame of mind. Remember, Sir, the state of political excitement at this moment. Remember the state of feeling between North and South; the contest between the slave power and the free power. Remember that this case is made a State issue by Virginia, a national question by the Executive. Reflect that every reading man in Virginia, with all the pride of the Old Dominion aroused in him, is turning his eyes to the result of this issue. No man could be more liable to bias than a Virginian, testifying in Massachusetts, at this moment, on such an issue, with every powerful and controlling motive on earth enlisted for success.

Take the other supposition, which may be the true one, that Mr. Brent does not know Anthony Burns particularly well. He goes down to Alexandria to tell Col. Suttle that he has escaped. The record is made up there, as best they can. Mr. Brent did not go there as a witness to identify, and does the best he can. He does not recollect whether he is a negro or mulatto, or of what shade, so he calls him "dark complexioned," and he can speak only of a scar, he does not know on which cheek and of a scar on the hand. Beyond this, he is uncertain. If this is so, your Honor can have no satisfying description of Anthony Burns, the slave of Col. Suttle, if such a person there be.

But there is, fortunately, one fact, of which Mr. Brent is sure. He knows that he saw this Anthony Burns in Richmond, Virginia, on the 20th day of March last, and that he disappeared from there on the 24th. To this fact, he testifies unequivocally. After all the evidence is put in on our side to show that the prisoner was in Boston on the 1st and 5th of March, he does not go back to the stand to correct an error, or to say that he may have been mistaken, or that he meant only to say that it was *about* the 20th and 24th. He persists in his positive testimony, and I have no doubt he is right and honest in doing so. He did see Anthony Burns in Richmond, Va., on the 20th day of March, and Anthony Burns was first missing from there on the 24th. But the prisoner was in Boston, earning an honest livelihood by the work of his hands, through the entire month of March, from the 1st day forward. Of this your Honor cannot, on the proofs, entertain a reasonable doubt.

William Jones, a colored man well known in this city, who works for the city, and for the Mattapan Company, and for others, and entirely unimpeached, testifies that on the first day of March he met the prisoner in Washington Street. He knows the man. He tells you of all the places he went to with him to find work for him to do. He received him into his house as a boarder on that day. On the 5th day of March they began working together at the Mattapan Works, in South Boston, cleaning windows and whitewashing, and worked for five or six days. Then, on the 18th they worked at the City Building. Then Burns left him for another employ. Jones cannot be mistaken as to the identity. The only question would be as to the truth of his story. It is a truth or it is a pure and sheer fabrication. I saw at once, and as every one must have felt, that the story so full of details, with such minuteness of dates and names and places, must either stand impregnable or be shattered to pieces. The fullest test had been tried. The other side has had a day in which to follow up the points of Jones's diary, and discover his errors and falsehoods. But he is corroborated in every point.

Mr. Drew, the clerk of the Mattapan Works, says that Jones and the prisoner cleaned the windows and did the whitewashing of that establishment from the 5th to the 10th of March. He has an entry of the first day's payment in his card book on the 5th. Various other payments were made at intervals, until the 28th, when a final settlement was had. This settlement included Jones's work in painting which went on after the window cleaning was done. He says that after he settled with Jones, the prisoner came to him to know how much he paid Jones for his work, and he told him. He says he heard that he was wanted as a witness, and thought it a joke, and came down here and was told that the man claimed as a slave had worked for him. He came into the room and recognized him at once, and the prisoner recognized the witness. His testimony corroborates Jones in another particular. Jones says he remembers the dates from the fact of a dispute between him and the prisoner, which led him to ask Mr. Russell to enter the dates of the prisoner's coming to his house in his pocket book, as Jones himself does not write. This pocket book was produced by Jones, and Mr. Russell, who made the entries, was sworn by us and has been here.

Mr. Whittemore is a member of the City Council, and was one of the Directors of the Mattapan Co. He made a journey to the West, from which he returned on the 8th day of March. On that day or the next, he went to the works, where his counting room is. The prisoner and Jones were cleaning the windows of the counting room. He noticed the peculiar condition of his hand, and the mark on his cheek. He is sure of the man and of the date. He heard at the armory of the Pulaski Guards, of which he is lieutenant, of Jones's testimony, and said to himself and others, "I shall know *that man*," and came here to see. As soon as he saw him, he knew him.

Now, Sir, Mr. Whittemore, in answer to a question from me, whether he was under the odium of being either a Free Soiler or an Abolitionist, said that he was a Hunker Whig. The counsel thought this an irrelevant question. I told him I thought it vital. Not that the political relations of Mr. Whittemore could affect your Honor's mind, but that it shows he has no bias on our side. Moreover, I am anxious not only that your Honor should believe our evidence, but that the public should justify you in so doing. And there is no fear but that the press and the public mind will be perfectly at ease if it knows that your Honor's judgment is founded even in part, in a fugitive slave case, in favor of the fugitive, on the testimony of a man who has such a *status illæsæ existimationis*, as a Hunker Whig, who is eke a train-band captain in a corps under arms!

Jones says that they went to work every day at 7 o'clock. Mr. Culver, the foreman, and Mr. Putnam, a machinist, and Mr. Gilman, the teamster, of the works, say that the hour of work was changed to 6 1-2 A. M., on the first of April. They also are quite sure, from the course of the work and their general recollection, that it was done early in March. Mr. Gilman has an additional recollection that it was a few days after pay day, which was March 1st. Mr. Putnam has a memorandum which shows that he began his own work there on the 3d or 4th day of March, and he says Jones began cleaning the windows a few days after.

Then Mr. Brown, one of the city Police, now on duty, testifies that on entering the Court Room, he recognized the prisoner at once. He has no doubt of him. He first saw him at the Mattapan Works cleaning windows with Jones. He himself left off his work there on the 20th of March, as his memorandum and recollection show. About ten days before he left off he changed his work to a new building in which there were no windows. The windows were cleaned in the old building and of course before the 10th of March. His attention was called to the man at the time. He spoke to him, and asked him to wash a certain window.

This is the testimony as to the Mattapan Works. Is it not conclusive? It is clear that the work was done there by Jones and a colored man from the 5th to the 10th of March. Jones worked there at no other time. This man was the prisoner. On a question of identity, numbers are every thing. One man may mistake, by accident, by design or bias. His sight may be poor, his observation imperfect, his opportunities slight, his recollection of faces not vivid. But if six or eight men agree on identity, the evidence has more than six or eight times the force of one man's opinion. Each man has his own mode and means and habits of observation and recollection. One observes one thing, and another another thing. One makes this combination and association, and another that. One sees him in one light or expression, or position, or action, and another in another. One remembers a look, another a tone, another the gait, another the gesture. Now if a considerable number of these independent observers combine upon the same man, the chances of mistake are lessened to an indefinite degree. What other man could answer so many conditions, presented in so various ways. On the point of the time and place, too, each of those witnesses is an independent observer. These are not links in one chain, each depending on another. They are separate rays, from separate sources, settling on one point.

Here we have the testimony of Mr. Favor, whom I know you have noticed as a respectable man, who remembers Jones bringing the prisoner to his shop, in Lincoln Street, to find work, very early in March; and Stephen Maddox. a tailor, says that Jones brought the prisoner to his shop to find work. He remembers telling him that he should have no work for him for two months, as his outdoor work, cleaning, &c.. did not begin so as to require help before the first of May. This is the natural observation, and it is as natural he should remember it. A poor man was applying for work. He was obliged to put him off, and, to show his sincerity, he explained to him the course of his work. He was obliged to sentence him to disappointment and delay for two months. He remembered it. It would be remembered by a kindly man, under such circumstances.

The attempt at contradiction as to the City Buildings fails. Mr. Gould confirms Jones's account that he worked there on the 18th or 17th of March. He does not recollect the prisoner being with him; but he admits that he was there only twice a day, and Jones said that the prisoner was there only an hour or so, to help him a little, without pay.

Mr. Brent puts his case resolutely and unequivocally on the ground that the man he means was in Richmond up to the 20th. We have proved that the prisoner was here on the 1st and 5th and 10th and 18th. This is inconsistent with the claimant's case. This witness does not pretend a mistake or doubt. They cannot pretend one in argument, because he has been in court all the while, and is not recalled.

If, we had the burden of proof, should we not. have met it? How much more then are we entitled to prevail, where we have only to shake the claimant's case by showing that it is left in reasonable doubt?

Whatever confidence I may have in this position, I must not peril the cause of my client by any overweening confidence in my own judgment. I must therefore call your Honor's attention to the other points of our defence.

Assuming now, for the purpose of further inquiry, that all our testimony is thrown out, and let the case rest on their evidence alone. It is incumbent on them to show that the prisoner owes service and labor to Col. Suttle, by the laws of Virginia, and that he escaped from that State into Massachusetts.

Does he owe service and labor to Col. Suttle?

The claimant, perhaps, will say that the record is conclusive on the facts of slavery and escape, and that the only point open is that of identity. That is so if he adopts the proper mode of proceeding to make it so. Section 10 of the Fugitive Slave Law provides a certain mode of proceeding, anomalous, in violation of all rules of common law, common right and common reason, a proceeding that has not its precedent, so far as I can learn, in the legislation of any Christian nation, therefore to be strictly construed, and not to be availed of unless strictly followed. It provides that the questions of slavery and escape shall be tried, *ex parte*, in the State from which the man escaped, and not in the State where he is found. The hearing and judgment are to be there and not here. This judgment being authenticated is to be produced here, and the Commissioner here has only jurisdiction to inquire whether the person arrested is the person named in the judgment. He cannot go into the matters there decided, but only see if the record fits the man.

Section 6 of the Statute provides an entirely different proceeding. It authorizes the Court here to try the questions of slavery and escape, as well as identity, and requires them to be tried by evidence taken here, or certified from the State from which he escaped, or both. It is not pretended that this transcript of a record is such evidence. Now, which proceeding are we under? Doubtless under that provided in the 6th section. The claimant introduces Mr. Brent, and by him offers evidence to prove the fact of slavery, the title of Col. Suttle, and the escape. He goes fully into these points. This was not offered as a mode of proving identity. The identity was proved first, and then the other evidence was put in. It was professedly to prove title and escape. Parts of it were objected to as not competent to prove those points, and advocated as competent for that purpose, and on no other ground, and ruled in or ruled out on that ground. They introduced evidence tending to show that a certain negro woman was a slave of Col. Suttle, and that that woman was the mother of Burns, and that his brothers and sisters are slaves, and they introduced evidence tending to show an escape, in the same manner. After that, they offered the record and we objected to it, and it was received *de bene esse*; and its admissibility is now to be decided upon.

We say that the two proceedings cannot be combined. The jurisdiction and duties of the magistrate are different in the two cases. The rights of parties are different. It is evident that the statute makes them different proceedings and not merely different proofs, for they are not merely put into separate sections, but each section contains a repetition of the foundation of a proceeding, its progress, the decision and execution, and each provides for the receiving of evidence of identity. There is a different form of certificate required in the two cases. On the face of the statute they are two proceedings. You cannot combine *scire facias* on a record with a count in assumpsit, proving the original debt by parol. You cannot, on the *voir dire* examine the party himself, and prove his interest by other evidence also.

Even if the record can be combined with parol proof, it can hardly be contended that it is conclusive against the proof the claimant himself puts with it. When the statute says it is conclusive, it means that the defendant is not admitted to contradict it by proof. But if the claimant introduces proof which overthrows its allegations, can he contend that it is conclusive? If he proves that the right to the certificate is in Millspaugh, and not in Col. Suttle, can he fall back on his record and claim a certificate for Col. Suttle? If he proves that the man did not escape, can he fall back on his record, and claim a certificate for an escaped fugitive?

I pray your Honor, earnestly, to confine this record—the venomous beast that carries the poison to life and liberty and hope in its fang—to confine it in the straitest limits. It deserves a blow at the hand of every man who meets it.

If your Honor considers the record as admissible, in other respects, and conclusive if admitted, we have objections to offer to it from the nature of its contents and form.

In the first place, it does not purport to be a "record of the matters proved." It is all in the way of recital. It says, "On the application of Chas. F. Suttle, who this day appeared and made satisfactory proof that, &c., it is ordered that the matters so proved and set forth be entered on the records of this Court," and there it ends. Well, have they entered the facts on the record? If so, I should like to see the entry. Where is the transcript of that record? All we have here is the porch to the building, with a superscription reciting what is to be found within. We are entitled to the building and its contents.

In the next place, the record does not, as I have already once observed, set forth a description of the person " with such convenient certainty as may be." It does not tell you whether he is a negro, a mulatto, a white, or an Indian. The rest of the description would be full enough, if it fitted the prisoner at the bar. That goes, to be sure, to the point of identity. But let me remind you, Sir, here, that a scar is not a large brand, and that a scar is no adequate description of the state or appearance of that man's hand.

The record is also objectionable, because it does not allege that he escaped into another State. Unless he has escaped *into another State*, the *casus fœderis* does not arise. And how is your honor to know that he did escape into another State. The only evidence you can legally receive is on the point of identity. If you proceed strictly by the record, you are without evidence of one great fact necessary to call into action the constitutional powers.

We have great confidence, please your Honor, that the record will be excluded on one or more of these points;. or that, if admitted, we may control it by the claimant's own testimony.

Does he then, by the claimant's own evidence, owe to Col. Suttle service and labor?

Their evidence shows conclusively that he does not. Mr. Brent tells us that Col. Suttle made a lease of him to a Mr. Millspaugh of Richmond, in January last, and that he was in the service of Mr. Millspaugh when he disappeared. It is the ordinary case of a lease of a chattel. The lessee has the temporary property and control. The reversioner has no right to interfere with the possession or direction of the chattel during the lease. This proceeding has always been defended, by those who hold it to be constitutional, on the ground that it merely secures and affects the temporary control of the slave, and does not affect the general property. It is not a judgment *in rem*. There is no decree affecting title. If this is so, there can be no pretence of a right on the part of the reversioner to the certificate prayed for here. A little consideration makes this clear. The claimant says he has escaped without leave, and asks for power to reduce him into possession and under control again — into his own possession and under his own control. Now, Mr. Millspaugh has the sole right of possession and control. Mr. Millspaugh may allow him to come to Massachusetts and stay here until the end of the lease, if he chooses. Col. Suttle has nothing to say about it. If Mr. Millspaugh does not return him to Col. Suttle at the end of his lease, he is liable to Col. Suttle on his bond, which Mr. Brent tells us is given in these cases. Suppose your Honor should grant the certificate, and Col. Suttle should take the man to Mr. Millspaugh, Mr. Millspaugh would say to him, "Why are you carrying my man about the country? I have not asked or desired you to do any such thing?"

"But," says Col. Suttle, "I have a certificate from a Commissioner in Boston certifying that he is now owing me service and labor, and authorizing me to take and carry him off."

"Then the Commissioner did not know that I had a lease of him."

"Yes he did, Mr. Brent let that out. It came very near upsetting our case. But we got our certificate, somehow or other, notwithstanding."

But no such answer will be given to any certificate to be issued by your Honor. On the contrary, when Col. Suttle goes back to Virginia and tells Mr. Millspaugh that he was refused the certificate, Mr. Millspaugh will say to him, "To be sure you were. Did you not know law enough to know, you and Brent together, that you had no right to the possession and control of the man I have hired on a lease. Did you suppose the Boston commissioners would have so little regard for this species of property in Virginia as to give it away to the first comer?"

Beside this lease, leaving only a reversion in Col. Suttle, the reversion itself is mortgaged. Mr. Brent told us, in his simplicity, thinking he was all the time proving prodigious acts of ownership, that Col. Suttle mortgaged Burns, with other property, to one Towlson. This mortgage has never been paid or discharged, so far as we know. The evidence leaves it standing. Even if the reversioner could otherwise have this certificate, he cannot here, for there is a mortgage. A mortgage of a chattel passes the legal property, so that the mortgagor cannot maintain trover for its conversion. (Holmes v. Bell, 3 Cush.)

There is greater need for adhering to this rule as to the right of present possession and control in this proceeding than in ordinary actions, for an *escape* is an essential element in the claimant's case. To constitute an escape, the fugitive must have gone away against the will of the person having a right to say whether he shall go or come. This person is the lessee. As Col. Suttle could not authorize Burns to leave Virginia, so neither could he forbid his leaving it. He has simply nothing to say about it. He cannot authorize him to stay in Massachusetts, nor can he compel him to go away. He may say that if he cannot, his reversion is good for nothing. That is the case with all leases of chattels. He should think of that when he parts with his property. He does provide for it. He takes a bond. If the man is not returned to him at the end of his lease, let him look to his bond! Let him not come here, to Massachusetts, disturb the peace of the nation, exasperate the feelings of our people to the point of insurrection by this revolting spectacle, summon in the army and navy to keep down by bayonets the great instincts of a great people, haul to prison our young men of education and character, and persecute them even unto strange cities, and cause the blood of a man to be shed. Let him look to his bond! If he must peril life, disturb peace, outrage feelings and exasperate temper from one end of the Union to the other, let him do it for something that belongs to him, not for a mortgaged reversion in a man. Let him look to his bond!

Mr. Millspaugh, who alone has the right, if any one, to institute these proceedings, has done nothing about them. They do not produce even his affidavit.

In the next place, setting aside the difficulty about the lease, and the mortgage, and the identity, has the man ever escaped? He is said to have escaped from the control and possession of Mr. Millspaugh. How do we know that? The only evidence is that of Mr. Brent, and what does Mr. Brent know about it? He only knows that he was in Richmond on the 20th, and was missing on the 24th. He does not even say that he has ever spoken to Mr. Millspaugh about it, or that Mr. Millspaugh was at home, or has complained about it. Mr. Millspaugh may have given him leave, or may not care whether he is away or not. There is no evidence of an escape. There is only evidence that he is missing. He was there. Now (for the argument, grant it) he is here. What of it? Did he come away of his own will, and against the will of Mr Millspaugh? Unless both these concur, there is no escape. There is no evidence on either point, except the evidence of the prisoner, which they have put in. Mr. Brent says that on the night of the arrest, Col. Suttle asked the prisoner how he came here. He replied that he was at work on board a vessel, became tired and fell asleep, and was brought off in the vessel. As they have put in this evidence, they are bound by it. This shows there was no escape, for it is the only evidence at all bearing upon the character of his act. Taking this to be true, as the claimants must, there is no *escape*. In Aves's case, 18 Pick., 193, and Sims's case, 7 Cushing, 285, it has been decided that the *escape* is the *casus fœderis* under the Constitution. No matter how the slave got here, if he did not voluntarily escape, against his master's will, unless both these elements concur, he cannot be taken back. Therefore the slave was held free, in a case where he and his master were both sent here by a superior power, in a public vessel. (Referred to in Sims's case.)

If there was any doubt about this matter of escape, the point should be determined against the claimant, because he has failed to produce proof within his power which would settle the matter. He has not produced the only man beside the fugitive who knows whether he did escape or not. If he could not produce him in person, if there be a Judge or a Justice of the peace in the Old Dominion, he could have brought his affidavit. He has had time to procure it since this trial began. He does not ask for a delay that he may procure it.

The only evidence, in this conflict, which can aid your Honor's judgment, is the evidence of the admission of the prisoner, made to Col. Suttle, on the night of the arrest. He was arrested suddenly, on a false pretence, coming home at nightfall from his day's work, and hurried into custody, among strange men, in a strange place, and suddenly, whether claimed rightfully or claimed wrongfully, he saw he was claimed as a slave, and his condition burst upon him in a flood of terror. This was at night. You saw him, Sir, the next day, and you remember the state he was then in. You remember his stupefied and terrified condition. You remember his hesitation, his timid glance about the room, even when looking in the mild face of justice. How little your kind words reassured him. Sir, the day after the arrest you felt obliged to put off his trial two days, because he was not in a condition to know or decide what he would do.

Now, you are called upon to decide his fate upon evidence of a few words, merely mumblings of assent or dissent, perhaps mere movings of the head, one way or the other, construed by Mr. Brent into assent or dissent, to questions put to him by Col. Suttle, put to him at the moment the terrors of his situation first broke upon him. That you have them correctly you rely on the recollections of one man, and that man testifying under incalculable bias. If he has misapprehended or misrepresented the prisoner in one respect he may in another. In one respect we know he has. He testifies that when Col. Suttle asked him if he wished to go back, he understood him to say he did. This we know is not true. The prisoner has denied it in every form. If he was willing to go back why did they not send to Coffin Pitts's shop, and tell the prisoner that Col. Suttle was at the Revere House, and would give him an opportunity to return. No, Sir, they lurked about the thievish corners of the streets, and measured his height and his scars to see if he answered to the record, and seized him by fraud and violence, six men of them, and hurried him into bonds and imprisonment. Some one hundred hired men, armed, keep him in this room, where once Story sat in judgment — now a slave pen. One hundred and fifty bayonets of the regulars, and fifteen hundred of the militia keep him without. If all that we see about us is necessary to keep a man who is willing to go back, pray sir, what shall we see when they shall get hold of a man who is not willing to go back?

I regret, extremely, that you did not, sir, adopt the rule that in the trial of an issue of freedom, the admissions of the alleged slave, made to the man who claims him, while in custody, during the trial, should not be received. That ruling would have been sustained by reason, and humanity, and precedent. Failing that, I hoped the facts of this case would show enough of intimidation to throw out the evidence. At least, they show enough to deprive it of all weight. I have reminded you of his condition the next morning. What must it have been there? One of his keepers, True, says he was that night a good deal intimidated. Who intimidated him? Do you recollect the significant words of Col. Suttle, "I make *no compromises* with you! I make you no promises and no threats." This means, It is according to the course you take now that you will be treated when I get you back. If you put me to no trouble and expense it will be few stripes or no stripes. If you do, it will be many stripes. Was ever man more distinctly told it would be better for him if he acquiesced in every thing, yielded every thing, assented to every thing? That is what those words, uttered in a tone, no doubt, that he well understood, conveyed to his mind. But I am wasting words. I know that your Honor will give little or no weight to testimony so liable, at all times, to misconception, misrecollection, perversion, and, in this case, so cruel to use against such a person under such circumstances.

You recognized, Sir, in the beginning, the presumption of freedom. Hold to it now, Sir, as to the sheet-anchor of your peace of mind as well as of his safety. If you commit a mistake in favor of the man, a pecuniary value, not great, is put at hazard. If against him, a free man is made a slave forever. If you have, on the evidence or on the law, the doubt of a reasoning and reasonable mind, an intelligent misgiving, then, Sir, I implore you, in view of the cruel character of this law, in view of the dreadful consequences of a mistake, send him not away, with that tormenting doubt on your mind. It may turn to a torturing certainty. The eyes of many millions are upon you, Sir. You are to do an act which will hold its place in the history of America, in the history of the progress of the human race. May your judgment be for liberty and not for slavery, for happiness and not for wretchedness; for hope and not for despair; and may be the blessing of Him that is ready to perish may come upon you.

THOMAS'S CLOSING ARGUMENT FOR THE CLAIMANT.

Seth J. Thomas, Esq., commenced his closing argument for the claimant. Having been occupied almost constantly in court since nine o'clock this morning, he would have preferred a night's repose before proceeding; but, as the defendant's counsel objected, he was ready and would now go on.

The counsel for the defendant commenced his closing argument with some congratulations to the court, the marshal, the city — to almost every body but to him, Mr. Thomas, and his learned associate. He, too, had some congratulations to offer; to the marshal, who had shown, in the discharge of his difficult and arduous duty, firmness, decision, prudence, and kindness to the defendant; to the presiding judge, who, hearing patiently all that had been submitted, had shown equal fairness and liberality to either side; to his learned associate, who, though differing from him in politics, had concurred with him at every step as to the duty of counsel. These, and more, he congratulated that they were about to be relieved from a service on which they had entered, not as volunteers, but from a sense of duty, and from which they could all retire with a consciousness that the blood of the murdered man did not at least rest on them. He would congratulate, also, the city of Boston, that order was supreme; that Faneuil Hall, that cradle of law as well as of liberty, was closed to-day against treasonable and insane speech; and that the Music Hall, too, was closed against blasphemy of Almighty God, and to charges of murder done by this court — made by one a day or two since, who, though not a lawyer, but claiming to be a minister of the gospel, has the assurance to come here within the bar and occupy a privileged seat.

The claimant in this case, Charles F. Suttle, says he is of Alexandria, in the State of Virginia; that, under the laws of that state, he held to service and labor one Anthony Burns, a colored man; that on or about the 24th day of March last, while so held to service by him, the said Anthony escaped from the said State of Virginia, and that he is now here in court. He prays you to hear and consider his proofs in support of this his claim, and, if they satisfactorily support it, that you will certify to him, under your hand and seal, that he has a right to transport him back to Virginia. This is his whole case; this is all that he asks you to do. Under your certificate he may take him back to the place from whence he fled; and he can, in virtue of that, take him no where else. Now, to entitle the claimant to this certificate, what must he prove? Two things. 1. That Burns owed service and labor to him, the claimant. 2. That he escaped. How is he to prove these? The statute answers. He may apply to any court of record in Virginia, or judge thereof, in vacation, and make satisfactory proof to such court or judge that Burns owes service or labor to him, and that he escaped. The court shall then cause a record to be made of the matters so proved, and also a general description of the person, with such convenient certainty as may be; and a transcript of such record, authenticated by the attestation of the seal of the court, being produced here, where the person is found, and, being exhibited to you, is to be taken by you as conclusive of the facts of escape and of service due. And upon the production by the claimant of other and further evidence, if necessary in respect of the identity of the person escaping, he is to be delivered up to the claimant, with a certificate of his right to take him back; or his claim may be heard upon other satisfactory proofs competent in law. Such are the requirements. How have we met them? We have put in the transcript of a record. It is duly authenticated, and is conclusive upon the court of the two facts therein recited; viz., that the claimant held one Anthony Burns to service or labor, and that he escaped. These two facts are not open here. Then the question remains, is the person at the bar, Anthony Burns, as he is called — nobody thinks of calling him any thing else — is he the Anthony Burns named in the record? If he is, there is an end of the case. The claim is made out, and the certificate must follow. This, with simple proof of identity, would have been all that, in an ordinary case, counsel would have deemed it necessary to do. But, in an extraordinary case like this, it was deemed by us fit to go further. And, in addition to the record and proof of identity, we have put in the testimony of Brent, who had known Burns from a boy, had had him in his own employ, and had leased him to others, for several years, during all which time Col. Suttle claimed to own him, and treated him in all respects as his slave. We put in also Burns' admissions that Col. Suttle was his master. How does it stand as to the question of identity? There is, first, the description in the record — a man of dark complexion, six feet high, with a scar on his face and another scar on his right hand, and about twenty-three or four years of age. The person at the bar is about six feet high, has a prominent scar on his cheek and a scar on his right hand, and appears about the age mentioned. It would be difficult to find another person among the whole colored population of Boston who so well answers the description as the person at the bar. The concurrence of all these marks in another would be extraordinary indeed. This is worth considering. The learned counsel complains of the expression dark complexion as not sufficiently certain, and objects to the record on that ground. There can be no doubt that he is of *dark* complexion — the suggestion is that he is very dark. It is certainly no misdescription, and is sufficiently exact. Then they say there is a fracture of one of the bones of the hand instead of a scar. But it is, nevertheless, a scar. But they say it cannot be the Anthony Burns described in the record, because this man was here on the first of March; whereas Brent says Colonel Suttle's Anthony Burns was in Richmond on the nineteenth or twentieth of March. It is, of course, clear that this man could not have been both here and in Virginia from the first to the nineteenth of March. To show that he was here, they have put into the case the testimony of one Jones, a colored man, and rely on that.

He undertakes to fix the time by a memorandum book, which he did not himself keep, which we have not examined, and which is not in the case. We believe that his story is manufactured for the case. He says he called on Col. Suttle, and learned from him that his man escaped on the 24th. Then he saw Burns at the window on Sunday, found he was the man who worked with him at South Boston on the fourth of March, and made up his mind that it was his duty to come here and swear so. And he has come. He tells us on whom he called with Burns, on the day when he first saw him. They ask us why we didn't call these men to contradict him. The answer is they have called most of them to support him; Maddocks was one of them, and his testimony is of the same class as Jones, coined at the same mint, made up at the same factory. The only one not of his class, was Gould. We called him, and he directly contradicts Jones. Jones undoubtedly did work at the Mattapan Works, and there was, no doubt, another colored man there with him. But it was not Burns. No doubt Whittemore saw Jones there, and perhaps on the day he named, and no doubt saw the other colored man also. But he never saw Burns there. He is mistaken in the man. That is all.

Drew, the clerk, whom they call to support Jones, and who they say does support him, so far from that, weakens his statement. He thinks it the same man. But he did not see the scar on his face; and since he thinks him the same man and didn't see it, he thinks his face was turned the other way. Who believes he kept it so turned? A juster inference would be, that since he did not see the scar it was not the same man. Yet Drew would have been more likely to notice the man that was there than any of the rest of them. Neither Drew nor Whittemore nor Favor nor any one of all those called to support Jones, has seen Burns since, nor had they ever seen him before.

The truth is, Jones went to them and asked them if they did not remember the man he had with him cleaning the windows; told them this was the man, impressed them with this fact. They came into court with this impression and made up their minds that he was. This is the only theory consistent with their honesty. Neither of them ever expected when they first saw him, to see him again; neither had any reason for taking notice of him. Whittemore on his examination in chief, did not swear that he saw the scar; on his cross examination he did. The reason is, that since he believed he saw the man, and saw now, that if he did see him he must have seen the scar, he thinks he saw the scar. The same may be said of all, with the exception of Maddocks. His is new coin. He says he recollects it, because he recollects what he said at the time. But it is incredible that he should have said what he now swears he did, and unlikely that he would have remembered it if he had.

Besides, Jones first saw this man on Washington street on the first day of March. He was a stranger. He stepped up to Jones and asked him if he could give him work. If he had been here before that, why ask a stranger such a question? He can't tell how he was dressed. They went to see Maddocks. That night Burns went home with Jones. Why, but because he was a stranger just arrived from Virginia? He staid with him the next day, and from that till the 18th. No doubt he did board with Jones as Jones states, but he has designedly fixed the date earlier than it was.

The learned counsel said we might press the fact that they gave no account of Burns before the first of March. He was right. Where did he come from? Where was he in February or January, or last year? Where was he born? Where has he been living? They say he may have come from New York or Cincinnati or Canada. True! But where did he come from? If he came from either of these, why name three; why not stick to one? He *may* have come from all, perhaps; but he *did* come from Richmond. So he says; so we say. But they say he may have sisters, fugitives, and brothers, too, and he had rather suffer than betray them. True. But if he had sisters in Canada, what harm could come to them by coming here and testifying that this man was born there? There has been time enough given to telegraph to either or all of these places; and the counsel have been grossly negligent in not doing it, if by so doing they might have delivered this man out of the peril in which they say he stands. The truth is, the sisters are all in Virginia.

They say these witnesses show that Brent is wrong in testifying that he saw Burns in Virginia on the 19th. Suppose this to be so; what then? The date is not material. A crime of a high nature, even, may be charged to have been done on the 24th of March, and proved to have been done on the 24th of February. But this is not a criminal charge, but a civil proceeding. There need be no formal complaint in the case. The complaint is merely the foundation for the warrant. The person escaping may be arrested without a warrant. Brent may possibly be mistaken in the date, but as to the identity of the person, he cannot be. Dates are easily mistaken unless marked by some particular fact. Brent says he last saw him on Sunday, the 19th. It may have been a Sunday or two previously, though I think he is right. They ask us why we did not recall him. We answer, we had no need to. He is as confident now as ever, and does not wish to change his testimony. But suppose Brent to be mistaken in the date; the fact of owing service and of escape remain, and if the identity is proved, the claim is nevertheless made out. As to the identity, the testimony of Brent, who had so long and well known him, is worth far more than all the rest, who but casually, if really at all, saw him. Here then is the man Anthony Burns, answering to the description in the record ; a man whose counsel can't account for before March — here is the testimony of Brent, and then comes, besides, the defendant's admissions — made not when in a state of intimidation, but when calm, and which correspond to the statements of Brent. Brent may possibly be mistaken — so may all the rest — but this unfortunate man cannot be. He knows. Brent, they say, is credible. He swears to the conversation up stairs, which shows that Burns knew him before then. How ?

The counsel read a portion of the first section of the 4th art. of the Constitution of the United States, but he did not read the whole of it. That article provided that Congress may prescribe the manner in which the judicial records of one State may be proved in another, and what effect they shall have. If Congress may do this, much more may it prescribe what shall be evidence in its own Courts, and what effect such records shall have there — which is all that it has undertaken to do in this case. This case then is proved in three ways — by the record, by the testimony of Brent, and by the admissions of the defendant — either of which ways would alone be sufficient. We have been asked why we didn't take the affidavit of Millspaugh.

The affidavit of Millspaugh as to the identity ? How was Millspaugh in Virginia to swear that this man here in Court was the man mentioned in the record ? And if for any other purpose, the answer is, we had better evidence, namely, the record — a judgment. They say this man owes service, not to Suttle, but to Millspaugh. But if he is the man described, that is not open to inquiry : and besides, Brent testifies the mortgage has been cancelled. What, then, remains, said Mr. T., but that you should grant to Col. Suttle a certificate ? It is said that, under your certificate, the man will not be carried to Virginia ; that he may be carried to Cuba or Brazil. They did not tell us how. If he is carried to Cuba, it will not be by authority of your certificate. And it would be difficult to show how a slave could be shipped from Boston to Brazil without his consent. The laws of the United States provide that a fugitive slave even cannot be shipped from one slave state to another by any vessel of more than forty tons burden without an entry being made at the custom house. It is said your certificate sends him into eternal bondage. It is only necessary to say in reply, it sends him to Virginia where he came from. When he gets back there, he will have the same rights he had before he came here. If the laws of that State don't sufficiently guard his rights, the fault is not yours nor mine. Those laws do, however, provide that slaves may institute trials for freedom, and the State pays the expenses of such trials. Your certificate has no effect upon his rights there. The late Mr. Justice Story, in the third vol. of his Commentaries on the Constitution, says, the Constitution contemplates summary ministerial proceedings, and not the ordinary course of judicial investigation to ascertain whether the claim be established beyond all legal controversy. Congress, he adds, appears to have acted upon this opinion ; and, accordingly, in the statute on this subject, have authorized summary proceedings before a magistrate upon which he may grant a warrant for a removal. As to the constitutionality of this statute, said Mr. T., it differs from that of '93 only in respect of the record, which has already been considered. The law of '93 has been pronounced constitutional by the highest judicial tribunal of the country ; and this law of 1850 has been held to be so by the Supreme Court of this State, all the judges concurring, and by every judge before whom a case under it has arisen. There I leave it. And if constitutional, and the claimant has a valid claim, why shouldn't he have the benefit of it ? What sort of a law is that which professes to protect one in his right of property, but which, when practically applied to a state of facts contemplated by it, from being objectionable to a class of persons, fails to secure such right ?

Here Mr. Thomas desired — as he had some other points which he wished to argue, and in view of the fact that the defence had occupied several days — that he might be allowed to finish his argument to-morrow. The Commissioner, however, said he was desirous of bringing the case to a close, and as the Circuit Court comes in to-morrow, the case must go on.

It remains, then, said Mr. T., only that I recapitulate the points already stated, and leave this arduous, and, in some respects, unpleasant case, in your hands. I am not conscious of having said or done any thing in the course of the examination that need have provoked personal hostility. If I have, it was not so intended. My connection with the case has been strictly professional. The extraordinary bitterness of opposing counsel has not changed my purpose or my direct course. The record is conclusive of two facts, that the person owed service and escaped. That record, with the testimony of Brent and the admissions, prove the identity. I take leave of the case, confident in the proofs presented, confident in the majesty of the law, and confident that the determination here will be just.

INCIDENTS OF THE LAST DAY.

As early as six o'clock this morning, a few persons had assembled in Court Square, evidently with the intention of remaining there at least until the decision of U. S. Commissioner Loring was made known, and, from that time, the crowd gradually increased.

Nine o'clock, A. M. The bell on the Court House has just tolled for the opening of the Commissioner's Court, and both the excitement and the crowd in the square are momentarily increasing, though there has been no direct breach of the peace. The larger portion of the crowd appear as if they were present from no other motive than that of curiosity. The notherly side of Court street is thronged with people, among whom are many females of every shade of complexion, apparently anxiously waiting to hear the announcement of the Commissioner's decision.

FIELD PIECE IN COURT SQUARE.

About half past seven o'clock this morning, a detachment of the 4th regiment U. S. Artillery, having previously been to the navy yard and received a field piece, marched up State street. The cannon was drawn by a pair of horses, and it was planted in Court square a little south of the easterly entrance of the Court House, and pointing towards Court street. Soon after, the Artillery were relieved by a detachment of U. S. Marines, who stood guard over the formidable piece of ordnance. Before eight o'clock several hundred persons had assembled in the square.

THE MILITARY.

The several companies of the M. V. M. in the city began to assemble at their respective armories at seven o'clock this morning, and soon after the streets resounded with the strains of martial music. The troops marched to the parade ground on the Common, where they formed into column, with the Lancers and Light Dragoons on the right, the whole under command of Maj. Gen. Edmands.

PRESENTATION TO THE FUGITIVE.

Last evening one of the U. S. Marshal's special officers started the generous project of procuring an entire new suit of clothes for Burns, the fugitive, and in a very short time the officers had contributed some $40, with which a handsome suit was purchased, and this morning Burns appeared in the court room dressed in a new and serviceable apparel. He expressed his warmest thanks to the officers for their generous and unexpected gift.

CLEARING THE SQUARE.

Half past nine o'clock, A. M. As soon as the announcement of the decision of the Commissioner was made known to the crowd on the easterly side of the Court House, the police cleared the Square of all persons, other than those who had special business within its limits.

A force of police was stationed at every avenue leading to the Square, with orders to admit none, except those whose business required them inside.

MOURNING DISPLAYED.

Hon. John C. Park has just displayed heavy folds of black cambric from each of the three windows of his office in Court square.

Several of the occupants of tenements on Court street are following the example set by Hon. Mr. Park, and are displaying folds of black on the outside of their stores and offices. Among the number are Messrs. Jacobs & Deane, A. N. Cook & Co., who have their awnings hung with festoons of black; J. A. Andrew, Esq., at the corner of Court and Washington street, also has the windows of his law office festooned in mourning.

The *Commonwealth* office presented three American flags, dressed in mourning, and lines of crape were stretched across the street.

Just after the military passed down State street, a coffin was produced and exhibited on the corner of State street, in front of the *Commonwealth* office. A struggle took place between those holding the coffin and the crowd, but the former retained possession of it.

The coffin was subsequently taken into the building and lowered out of one of the windows, with the inscription of " Liberty " on it.

COURT STREET.

Court street in front of the Court House and in the immediate vicinity, is filled with a mass of living beings.

ARTILLERY PRACTICE.

Ten o'clock, A. M. The U. S. Artillery have just been practising loading and firing (without discharging) their field piece in the square, with a degree of quickness and skill which gave all who witnessed their movements to understand that they were proficients in their business.

STATE STREET.

Large numbers of people are thronging the sidewalks in State street, evidently expecting every moment to see Burns pass down the street on his way to the vessel, which it is rumored and believed is to carry him back to Virginia.

OFFICERS TO ACCOMPANY BURNS.

Deputy U. S. Marshal John H. Riley, together with officers George J. Coolidge, Asa O. Butman, Charles Godfrey, and William Black have been detailed to accompany Burns on his passage to Virginia.

PROCLAMATION BY THE MAYOR.

His Honor, Mayor Smith, has issued the following proclamation, which has been posted about the streets :

PROCLAMATION! *To the Citizens of Boston.* To secure order throughout the City this day, Major General Edmands, and the Chief of Police, will make such disposition of the respective forces under their commands, as will best promote that important object; and they are clothed with full discretionary powers to sustain the laws of the land.

All well disposed citizens, and other persons, are urgently requested to leave those streets which it may be found necessary to clear temporarily, and under no circumstances to obstruct or molest any officer, civil or military, in the lawful discharge of his duty. J. V. C. SMITH, Mayor.

Mayor's Office, City Hall, Boston, June 2, 1854.

MAJOR GENERAL EDMANDS'S COMMAND.

The Line on the Common was formed, as before stated, and was composed of the following Battalions and Regiments, under command of Maj. Gen. B. F. Edmands :

First Battalion Light Dragoons, Maj. T. J. Pierce ; Co. A, (National Lancers,) Capt. Wilmarth.

Co. B, (Boston Light Dragoons,) Capt. Wright.

5th Reg't Artillery, Col. Robert Cowdin ; Co. A, (Boston Artillery,) Capt. Evans.

Co. B, (Columbian Artillery,) Capt. Cass.

Co. C, (Washington Artillery,) Capt. ———.

Co. D, (Roxbury Artillery,) Capt. Burrell.

Co. E, (American Artillery,) Capt. Granger.

Co. F, (Webster Artillery,) Capt. McCafferty.

Co. G, (Bay State Artillery,) Capt. Hincks.

Co. H, (Shields Artillery,) Capt. Young.

5th Reg't Light Infantry — Col. Charles L. Holbrook : Co. A, (Boston Light Infantry,) Capt. Rogers.

Co. B, (New England Guards,) Capt. Henshaw.

Co. C, (Pulaski Guards,) Capt. Wright.

Co. D, Boston Light Guard,) Capt. Follett.

Co. E, (Boston City Guards,) Capt. French.

Co. F, (Independent Boston Fusileers,) Capt. Cooley.
Co. G, (Washington Light Guard,) Capt. Upton.
Co. H, (Mechanic Infantry,) Capt. Adams.
3d Battalion Light Infantry, Maj. Robert I. Burbank; Co. A, (National Guard,) Lieut. Harlow, commanding.
Co. B, (Union Guards,) Capt. Brown.
Co. C, (Sarsfield Guards,) Capt. Hogan.
Cadets — Divisionary Corps of Independent Cadets, Lieut. Col. Thomas C. Amory, commanding.

EFFORTS TO PURCHASE BURNS.

Efforts have been making during the whole forenoon to purchase Burns, but they have been unsuccessful. We understand that those who here represent Colonel Suttle, will listen to no propositions until the fugitive is placed on board the cutter. To this Burns' friends demur, and in this position the matter stood at half past one.

The arrangements for Burns' return are said to be these. He is to be taken from the Court House and marched to the end of Long Wharf, and from thence put on board the revenue cutter Morris. The steamer John Taylor will tow the cutter to sea.

ARRESTS, &c.

Several arrests have been made during the forenoon. One man was arrested with two pistols in his possession, and was locked up in the Centre watch house. Two others were locked up for not obeying the orders of the police to clear the streets.

THE APPEARANCE OF STATE STREET.

The shutters of the stores on State street were closed and business was completely suspended after ten o'clock this forenoon. Crowds congregated on the corners, but the street was kept comparatively clear by the military and police.

ARREST OF ONE OF THE WITNESSES.

Jones, one of the witnesses in the slave case, was particularly earnest in his declamatory appeals on State street, and the disturbance which he created finally forced the police to take him in custody.

THE LATEST.

At two o'clock P. M., when our paper went to press, Burns had not been moved from the Court House.

The excitement had increased to the highest pitch.

The buildings on State street were crowded, and the military were on the alert and ready for duty at a moment's warning.

There can be no doubt that the fugitive will be conveyed on board the vessel, and it is to be hoped that his release by purchase will there be effected.

THE DECISION OF COMMISSIONER LORING.

The issue between the parties arises under the U. S. Statute of 1850, and for the respondent it is urged that the statute is unconstitutional. Whenever this objection is made it becomes necessary to recur to the purpose of the statute. It purports to carry into execution the provision of the constitution which provides for the extradition of persons held to service or labor in one State and escaping to another. It is applicable, and it is applied alike to bond and free — to the apprentice and the slave, and in reference to both, its purpose, provisions and processes are the same.

The arrest of the fugitive is a ministerial, and not a judicial act, and the nature of the act is not altered by the means employed for its accomplishment. When an officer arrests a fugitive from justice or a party accused, the officer must determine the identity, and use his discretion and information for the purpose. When an arrest is made under this statute, the means of determining the identity are prescribed by the statute; but when the means are used and the act done, it is still a ministerial act. The statute only substitutes the means it provides for the discretion of an arresting officer, and thus gives to the fugitive from service a much better protection than a fugitive from justice can claim under any law.

If extradition is the only purpose of the statute and the determination of the identity is the only purpose of these proceedings under it, it seems to me that the objection of unconstitutionality to the statute, because it does not furnish a jury trial to the fugitive, is answered; there is no provision in the Constitution requiring the *identity* of the person to be arrested should be determined by a jury. It has never been claimed for apprentices nor fugitives from justice, and if it does not belong to them it does not belong to the respondent.

And if extradition is a ministerial act, to substitute in its performance, for the discretion of an arresting officer, the discretion of a Commissioner instructed by testimony under oath, seems scarcely to reach to a grant of judicial power, within the meaning of the U. S. Constitution. And it is certain that if the power given to and used by the Commissioner of U. S. Courts under the statute is unconstitutional — then so was the power given to, and used by magistrates of counties, cities, and towns, and used by the act of 1793. These all were Commissioners of the United States — the powers they used under the statute were not derived from the laws of their respective States, but from the statute of the United States. They were commissioned by that and that alone. They were commissioned by the class instead of individually and by name, and in this respect the only difference that I can see between the acts of 1793 and 1850 is, that the latter reduced the number of appointees, and confined the appointment to those who by their professional standing should be competent to the performance of their duties, and who bring to them the certificates of the highest judicial tribunals of the land.

It is said the statute is unconstitutional, because it gives to the record of the Court of Virginia an effect beyond its constitutional effect. The first section of the fourth article of the Constitution is directory only on the State power and as to the State Courts, and does not seek to limit the control of Congress over the tribunals of the United States or the proceedings therein. Then in that article the term "records and judicial proceedings" refers to such *inter partes* and of necessity can have no application to proceedings avowedly *ex parte*. Then if the first section includes this record, it expressly declares as to "records and judicial proceedings," that Congress shall prescribe "*the effect thereof*," and this express power would seem to be precisely the power that Congress has used in the Statute of 1850.

Other constitutional objections have been urged here, which have been adjudged and readjudged by the Courts of the United States, and of many of the States, and the decisions of these tribunals absolve me from considering the same questions further than to apply to them the determination of the Supreme Court of this State in Sim's case, 7 Cushing, 309, that they "are settled by a course of legal decisions which we are bound to respect, and which we regard as binding and conclusive on the Court."

But a special objection has been raised to the record that it describes the escape as *from* the State of Virginia and omits to describe it as *into another State* in the words and substance of the Constitution. But in this the record follows the 10th section of the Statute of 1850, and the context of the section confines its action to cases of escape from one State, &c., into another, and is therefore in practical action and extent strictly conformable to the Constitution.

This Statute has been decided to be constitutional by the unanimous opinion of the Judges of the Supreme Court of Massachusetts on the fullest argument and the maturest deliberation, and to be the law of Massachusetts as well as, and because it is, a constitutional law of the United States; and the wise words of our revered Chief Justice in that case, 7 Cushing, 318, may well be repeated now, and remembered always. The Chief Justice says: —

"Slavery was not created, established, or perpetuated by the Constitution; it existed before; it would have existed if the Constitution had not been made. The framers of the Constitution could not abrogate Slavery, or the rights claimed under it. They took it as they found it, and regulated it to a limited extent. The Constitution, therefore, is not responsible for the origin or continuance of Slavery — the provision it contains was the best adjustment which could be made of conflicting rights and claims, and was absolutely necessary to effect what may now be considered as the general pacification, by which harmony and peace should take the place of violence and war. These were the circumstances, and this the spirit in which the constitution was made — the regulation of slavery so far as to prohibit States by law from harboring fugitive slaves was an essential element in its formation, and the Union intended to be established by it was essentially necessary to the peace, happiness, and highest prosperity of all the States. In this spirit and with these views steadily in prospect, it seems to be the duty of all judges and magistrates to expound and apply these provisions in the constitution and laws of the United States; and in this spirit it behooves all persons, bound to obey the laws of the United States, to consider and regard them."

It is said that the statute, if constitutional, is wicked and cruel. The like charges were brought against the act of 1793; and C. J. Parker, of Massa

,husetts, made the answer which C. J. Shaw cites and approves, viz : —
' Whether the statute is a harsh one or not, it is not for us to determine."

It is said that the statute is so cruel and wicked that it should not be exe-
:uted by good men. Then into what hands shall its administration fall, and
in its administration what is to be the protection of the unfortunate men who
are brought within its operation? Will those who call the statute merciless
commit it to a merciless judge?

If the statute involves that right, which for us makes life sweet, and the
want of which makes life a misfortune, shall its administration be confined
to those who are reckless of that right in others, or ignorant or careless of
the means given for its legal defence, or dishonest in their use? If any
men wish this, they are more cruel and wicked than the statute, for they
would strip from the fugitive the best security and every alleviation the
statute leaves him.

I think the statute is constitutional, as it remains for me now to apply it to
the facts of the case.

The facts to be proved by the claimant are three : —
1. That Anthony Burns owed him service in Virginia.
2. That Anthony Burns escaped from that service.

These facts he has proved by the record which the statute, sec. 10, declares " shall be held and taken to be full and *conclusive* evidence of the
fact of escape, and that the service or labor of the person escaping is due
to the party in such record mentioned."

Thus these two facts are removed entirely and absolutely from my jurisdiction, and I am entirely and absolutely precluded from applying evidence
to them. If therefore there is in the case evidence capable of such application, I cannot make it.

The 3d fact is the identity of the party before me with the Anthony
Burns mentioned in the record.

This identity is the only question I have a right to consider. To this,
and to this alone, I am to apply the evidence ; and the question whether the
respondent was in Virginia or Massachusetts at a certain time, is material only
as it is evidence on the point of identity. So the parties have used it, and the
testimony of the complainant being that the Anthony Burns of the record was
in Virginia on the 19th of March last, the evidence of the respondent has been
offered to show that he was in Massachusetts on or about the first of March
last, and thereafter till now.

The testimony of the claimant is from a single witness, and he standing
in circumstances which would necessarily bias the fairest mind — but other
imputation than this has not been offered against him, and from any thing
that has appeared before me, cannot be. His means of knowledge are personal, direct, and qualify him to testify confidently, and he has done so.

The testimony on the part of the respondent is from many witnesses
whose integrity is admitted, and to whom no imputation of bias can be attached by the evidence in the case, and whose means of knowledge are
personal and direct, but in my opinion less full and complete than that of
Mr. Brent.

Then between the testimony of the claimant and respondent there is a
conflict, complete and irreconcilable. The question of identity on such a

conflict of testimony is not unprecedented nor uncommon in judicial proceedings, and the trial of Dr. Webster furnished a memorable instance of it.

The question now is, whether there is other evidence in this case which will determine this conflict. In every case of disputed identity there is one person always whose knowledge is perfect and positive, and whose evidence is not within the reach of error, and that is the person whose identity is questioned, and such evidence this case affords. The evidence is of the conversation which took place between Burns and the claimant on the night of the arrest.

When the complainant entered the room where Burns was, Burns saluted him, and by his *Christian* name — "How do you do, Master CHARLES?" He saluted Mr. Brent also, and by his *Christian name* — "How do you do, Master *William?*" (To the appellation "Master," I give no weight.)

Col. Suttle said, "How came you here?" Burns said an accident had happened to him — that he was working down at Roberts's, on board a vessel — got tired and went to sleep, and was carried off in the vessel.

Mr. S. Anthony, did I ever whip you?

B. No sir.

Mr. S. Did I ever hire you out any where where you did not wish to go?

B. No sir.

Mr. S. Have you ever asked me for money that I did not give it to you?

B. No sir.

Mr. S. When you were sick did I not prepare you a bed in my own house, and put you upon it, and nurse you?

B. Yes sir.

Something was said about going back. He was asked if he was willing to go back, and he said — Yes, he was.

This was the testimony of Mr. Brent. That a conversation took place was confirmed by the testimony of Caleb Page, who was present, and added the remark that Burns said he did not come in Capt. Snow's vessel. The cross-examination of Brent showed that Col. Suttle said — "I make you no promises, and I make you no threats."

To me this evidence, when applied to the question of indentity, confirms and establishes the testimony of Mr. Brent in its conflict with that offered on the part of the respondent, and then on the whole testimony my mind is satisfied beyond a reasonable doubt of the identity of the respondent with the Anthony Burns named in the record.

It was objected that this conversation was in the nature of admissions, and that too of a man stupefied by circumstances and fear, and these considerations would have weight had the admissions been used to establish the truth of the matters to which they referred, i. e. the usage — the giving of money — nursing, &c.; but they were used for no such purpose, but only as evidence in reference to identity. Had they been procured by hope or fear, they would have been inadmissible; but of that I considered there was no evidence.

On the law and facts of the case, I consider the claimant entitled to the certificate from me which he claims.

As soon as the decision was rendered, the court room was cleared of all the spectators, to allow the necessary preparations to be made for the sending back of the fugitive.

Court Square was also cleared of the crowds which thronged it.

Every window overlooking the square was filled with at least a dozen heads of persons anxious to witness the poor fugitive when he should be brought out. Among the spectators were several ladies

At ten o'clock a detachment of the Dragoons passed up Court street, and were received with groans and hisses, and cries of " shame, shame," &c.

The business in the different courts was suspended while the preparations were going on to send the man back.

R. H. DANA, the senior counsel for the defence, passed out of the square about 11 o'clock, and as soon as the crowd saw him he was greeted with twelve hearty cheers.

BURNS'S EMBARKMENT.

AFTER our regular edition went to press, the Police, under Chief Taylor and Deputy Ham, cleared Court street, in front of the Court House, preventing the passage of omnibuses and other vehicles, and keeping the crowd of those on foot on the west of the Court House, west of the westerly avenue leading into the square from Court street.

Every avenue leading to Court street was guarded by detachments from Gen. Edmands's command, who, after leaving the Common, marched down Beacon and Tremont streets, through Court street, into State street — every avenue leading into which street received a detachment of the M. V. M., to guard against the ingress or egress of disorderly persons.

By adoping these means, the streets leading to Long wharf were kept comparatively clear of the thousands who had assembled, and this order was maintained until the end.

Subsequently the Cadets, National Guards, and Union Guards, marched back, up State and Court street, into Court square.

The Lancers were stationed for some hours in Court square, and from time to time sections were detailed to different parts of the streets through which it was expected that Burns would be taken, either to relieve the Light Dragoons or other companies who were on duty along State street, or for some other special purpose.

As Major Gen. Edmands and Staff entered Court square, they were greeted with applause by some and hisses by others. The cheers predominated, however.

As the preparations for the removal of Burns from the Court House were being consummated, a detachment of the Fourth Regiment United States Artillery was placed in charge of the " field piece," and cartridges were deposited in pouches which were borne by some of the men.

The United States troops, including both the Fourth Regiment Artillery, and the United States Marines, from Forts Independence and Constitution, were marched out of the Court House into the square, and each man's musket was duly inspected.

Next came out of the Court House, under command of Capt. Peter Dunbar, Jr., one hundred and twenty special officers, employed by the United States Authorities, who formed a hollow square, directly in front of the easterly entrance to the Court House.

This body of special aids was well armed, each man with a drawn Roman sword on his right side, and a loaded revolver in his belt at his left side. Upon their appearance, they were greeted with cheers, groans, hisses, and other manifestations of approval or detestation.

These preparations having been completed, Burns was escorted out of the Court House by United States Marshal Freeman and some half dozen of his aids, who took their position in the centre of the hollow square. At this moment Burns appeared as indifferent as the most uninterested spectator, and the cries of Shame! shame! the hisses, groans, and other demonstrations which greeted his appearance, did not seem in the least to excite him.

The column was then formed in the following order: A detachment of the National Lancers on the right and left of the street; a corps of United States Artillery, followed by a corps of United States Marines; hollow square of special officers, in the centre of which was the United States Marshal, his aids, and the fugitive, Anthony Burns; a corps of United States Marines; the field piece, drawn by a span of horses and manned by a detachment of six of the members of the Fourth Regiment United States artillery; a corps of United States Marines.

The rabble attempted to force their way upon the rear of the corps of United States Marines, but the formidable appearance of a detachment of the National Lancers, and others of the M. V. M., deterred them at short notice from proceeding.

At the corner of Court Square and Court street, the demonstrations were loud and uproarious.

Passing down State street the procession was greeted the whole entire route with mingled groans, cheers, and hisses, but no attempt at rescue was made. The most intense interest was manifested to get a parting glimpse of the fugitive.

As the column was passing through State street, by the office of the *Commonwealth*, the procession was greeted with a shower of cayenne pepper, cowitch, or some other most noxious substance, thrown from the *Commonwealth* building.

A bottle, containing a liquid, believed to be vitriol, was also thrown from the *Commonwealth* building, nearly across State street. The missile would have struck Joseph W. Coburn, Esq., had he not chanced to see it coming directly towards his head, and dodged aside. As it was, however, the bottle struck the pavement and was dashed in pieces, and very fortunately its contents harmed no one.

The procession turned at the head of Long Wharf and proceeded down the back side of the wharf and thence to T wharf, at which the steamer

John Taylor was lying. Burns was marched directly aboard and taken to the cabin out of sight of the crowd.

The wharves and vessels in the vicinity were crowded with thousands of persons gathered to witness the embarkation. The United States Marines and the company of United States troops from Fort Independence went down the harbor in the steamer.

The steamer was delayed at the wharf about one hour after Burns went on board. The delay was mainly occasioned by the labor of getting the field piece, which was drawn in the procession, aboard the steamer.

At quarter past three, every thing was on board, and the word to cast off was given. At precisely twenty minutes past three, the steamer swung from the wharf, and proceeded down the harbor, with Revenue Cutter Morris, which had previously been towed down to the Castle.

CPSIA information can be obtained at www.ICGtesting.com
Printed in the USA
LVOW03s1940230114

370707LV00022B/1011/P